D1130684

Paths To Jewish Belief

PATHS TO JEWISH BELIEF

A Systematic Introduction

By EMIL L. FACKENHEIM

Illustrated by CHET KALM

BEHRMAN HOUSE, INC. • PUBLISHERS • NEW YORK

LIBRARY — LUTHERAN SCHOOL
OF THEOLOGY AT CHICAGO

BM
600
.F3
1970

Seventh Printing, 1970

Copyright 1960 by Emil L. Fackenheim
Published by Behrman House, Inc., 1261 Broadway, New York 1
Manufactured in the United States of America
Library of Congress Catalog Card Number: 60-13856

To
My Father
AND THE MEMORY
of My Mother

ACKNOWLEDGEMENTS

A first version of this book was used and tested during the years 1953-56, in grade 10, the confirmation year of Holy Blossom Temple Religious School, Toronto. It benefited greatly from the criticisms of the students and from the encouragement of the senior rabbi, Dr. Abraham L. Feinberg, and of the director of education, Heinz Warschauer. Additional helpful suggestions were received from the following, who read the manuscript wholly or in part:

Rabbi Eugene Borowitz, Mrs. Eugene Borowitz, Rabbi Herman Schaalman, Rabbi Samuel M. Silver, Rabbi Morrison D. Bial, Rabbi Emanuel Green, Rabbi Bernhard N. Cohn, Heinz Warschauer, and my wife, Rose. The following helped prepare the manuscript for publication: Adam Margoshes and Ellen Rudin, who gave invaluable aid in simplifying and clarifying what were often a philosopher's much too complex and obscure thought and language; and Jacob Behrman, who acted tirelessly as the book's best friend and severest critic.

CONTENTS

You have probably read enough about different religions to know that they believe different things. But if you had done no reading in the subject, you would still know from experience that Christianity differs in important points from Judaism. Even if you had never met a Christian whose beliefs differ from yours, you would still be aware that Jews differ among themselves—for you know that there are Orthodox, Conservative and Reform Jews. You may even know some people who say they believe nothing at all.

Such disagreement is troubling. It isn't like disagreeing on the best kind of sport. If you like football and your friend likes hockey, there is no reason why you both can't be right. Both games are good games. You simply prefer one to the other. But religious beliefs are quite another matter. When a person believes in One God, he is not just saying that he likes this belief better than the belief in many gods. He is saying that he thinks his belief is true. And he cannot possibly admit that the belief in many gods is just as true for someone else as the belief in One God is for himself.

One can't be like the rabbi in the old joke. Two congregants came to him to let him judge a dispute in religious belief. The rabbi first heard one and said to him, "You are right." Then he heard the second and told him that he, too, was right. Finally, someone who had listened said, "But, rabbi, they can't both be right." Whereupon the rabbi said, "You are right!"

The rabbi of this joke was being tolerant. But he was showing the wrong kind of tolerance. He should have told both congregants that they were entitled to their belief, but he shouldn't have acted as if both beliefs could be true at the same time. The same applies to all of us. We must never forget that every man is entitled to his religious belief. But if we act as if all religious beliefs can be equally true, no matter how much they differ, then we are saying that no one of the beliefs is true at all.

One conclusion which follows from this is that if a person has a faith that means anything to him, he can only passionately stick to it, despite the fact that not everyone agrees with him. In fact, nothing great has ever been achieved without this kind of faith, and a very great example of this is our Jewish history. At one time, our ancestors lived in a pagan world wholly in disagreement with their faith. Yet they passionately stuck to it. Had they not done so, we should certainly not be here today. And it is most likely that the world would still be pagan.

But this is only one conclusion. People often have passionate beliefs in foolish things, such as in the protective power of a rabbit's foot. What would we say if such people told us that it is right to believe in a rabbit's foot and absurd to believe in God? Any intelligent neutral observer would concede that the belief in a rabbit's foot is absurd; but he wouldn't say that the belief in God is absurd, even if he did not share it himself. Or again, people sometimes passionately believe in vicious things, such as in the destruction of a certain race. But any ordinary decent person, even a person without religious belief, would know that this is vicious and terribly wrong.

These examples suggest that we must not accept our beliefs on faith alone, but must also examine them in the light of reason. Such an examination can accomplish three things. First, it can help us eliminate from our beliefs the childishness and superstitions that keep creeping into all religions, the Jewish included. Second, it can help bring about a measure of agreement among intelligent and well meaning people of different faiths. And third, it can help bring us to a better understanding of our own faith.

Some people would add still a fourth thing that reason can do; they say it can *prove* our religious beliefs just as we can often prove our scientific beliefs. But this is going too far. If we could prove our religious beliefs, then all intelligent people would agree about religion just as they do about science when something can be proved. Of course this isn't so.

Of the above accomplishments, the third is the most important. When as children we are first instructed in our religion, we are much too young to understand it. We come to accept certain beliefs, but we don't know why we believe them. We don't really understand what we believe. So when we grow older and begin to think about things, we often come to doubt our beliefs as being unreasonable or even downright childish.

Now many of our beliefs may in fact be childish. But others only *seem* childish because, not understanding them fully, we have accepted them in a childish form. Yet until we have examined them, how can we know which are which? How can we know what to keep on believing and what not to believe in any more?

Sometimes people are afraid to examine their beliefs in this way. They feel that once you start questioning one belief, you will end up rejecting all of them, and that the only way to believe is to believe blindly and shut all questions out. But they are quite wrong; there is no need to be afraid. Judaism has never been afraid of rational examination. Judaism has always believed that God gave us a mind with which to think as well as a heart with which to believe, and that He meant us to make use of both.

In this book we are going to look at the main beliefs of Judaism, with a view to deciding for ourselves what we can and what we cannot accept.

PART ONE

GOD

We have seen the importance of reason in justifying our belief in Judaism. Now our first question must be about God. Is there a God? Does everyone believe in God? What do people believe in who do not believe in God? What shows us that there is a God? Can we be sure? How does Judaism answer these questions?

"Just as the clock is evidence for a clock-maker, the universe is evidence for a universe-maker—for God."

RELIGION is the worship of God. As we all know, religions differ a great deal about God, man and the universe. But they also agree unanimously on some basic beliefs. Every religion believes in the existence of God.

Religion Must Have a God

Is God concerned with man? What is the relationship between man and God? Did God create man to have free will? There are many such questions, and for each question there are many answers. But for the most important question, the very first question—Is there a God?—the answer is the same for all religions.

If religions did not believe in God, to whom would we pray? When we took our deepest troubles to God in prayer, no one would be listening. For many men this might be a tragedy. For the religious man it is an impossibility. Because when the religious man prays, he feels the presence of God; he knows there is a God who listens to him.

This is the central faith that makes religion religion. It is because religion connects us with God that it has always been supremely important to people everywhere.

Theists, Atheists and Agnostics

People who believe in God, whatever their religion, are called *theists*. People who believe that there is no God are called *atheists*. And people who believe that we cannot decide whether or not God exists are called *agnostics*. In a way, agnostics have the easiest intellectual position to defend. They don't have to prove anything, because they don't assert anything. They merely say that the existence of God has not been proved. They say, "Show me."

Man's thinking about God is the subject of an interesting story by the great Czech-Jewish writer, Franz Kafka. In this story—supposed to be written by a dog—the human race is invisible to the dogs, just as God is invisible to you and me.

In the story, the great question of dog philosophy is where their food comes from. The oldest dogs say that it comes from above, from unseen powers. The young dogs say that because they can't see where the food comes from, its appearance must be a matter of chance. Finally, a third group of dogs say that there is not enough evidence to decide one way or the other. The old dogs are the *theists*, the young dogs are the *atheists* and the uncertain dogs are the *agnostics*.

Agnosticism is a very common attitude today. If you have ever talked about the existence of God with your friends, you have probably been asked, "If God exists, where is He? Why can't I see Him or hear Him or touch Him? And if He cannot be seen or heard or touched, then how can we know that He exists?"

People have always asked these questions, but they ask them more often and more insistently today. The main reason for this questioning is the growth of science and the acceptance of the scientific method. Scientific method works, and therefore it is deeply respected—as it should be. But some people feel that only scientifically proved things can be true. However, this is a mistake.

The unprovability of the theist position is not a scientific argument against it. We don't mean to say that the theist's arguments are scientific. But there is nothing unscientific about them either.

Most of the theoretical proofs of modern science rest on a high degree of probability—not certainty. One of the cornerstones of modern physics is the uncertainty principle. According to this principle, we can never make exact measurements of both the speed and location of subatomic particles. If the speed is exact, the location is uncertain; and if the location is exact, the speed is uncertain. Therefore we can only know the probable speed and location of a particular particle at any given moment.

Another good illustration of scientific uncertainty is the present state of the theory of light. Is light, like matter, composed of particles? Or is it a vibration of waves? The two theories seem to contradict each other, but, in practice, physics uses both. Sometimes light is treated one way, sometimes the other way.

The reasoning behind belief in God must be unusually convincing. It has been accepted by the vast majority of men at all times, including most of the greatest philosophers and scientists from Plato to Einstein. There are very few other ideas, if any, which have achieved such widespread acceptance. Surely the agreement of so many thinkers from such different environments must be based on solid foundations.

The Wonder of the Universe

The biggest and most obvious argument for theism is the physical universe—not just the earth, but the whole cosmos, which includes the solar system, the stars and all the galaxies. If the universe were nothing but a whirling mass of atoms, we would expect to find complete chaos. But instead, wherever we look, we see the evidence of order.

It is easy to take the setting and the rising of the sun for granted, and to ignore the nightly movement of the stars. It is easy for us to accept these daily miracles without wonder and without thought, because they are always with us and always have been. They are the eternal, unchanging background of the transient, changing events of human history.

But in the life of every man, no matter how busy he may be, come moments of quiet reflection. And every man, no matter how hard or "practical" he may be, has moments of deep feeling, of being in touch with the world of nature. In these moments, every one of us has felt an awe, a wonder, at the majestic regularity of the movements of the stars in their courses. It is such moments which first gave rise to the religious conviction that the cosmic order can only be explained by a cosmic Creator.

From the beginning of human thought, cosmic order has been used as an argument for theism. It is perhaps the oldest argument, but still one of the best. The following classic story helps to show its power:

A man is shipwrecked on a desert island and is convinced that he is the only man there. But one day, while walking on the beach, he finds a clock lying in the sand. He is filled with hope, because now he knows that the island has been visited by other men.

Now the universe we find ourselves in is an infinitely more complex and more wonderful construction than a clock. Is it likely, as the atheists maintain, that while the clock was made for a purpose and according to a craftsman's design, the universe is only an accidental collection of atoms? Only an insane person would say this about the clock.

True, no one has ever seen the maker of the universe. But the shipwrecked sailor did not have to see the clock-maker to believe he existed. Just as the clock is evidence for a clock-maker, the universe is evidence for a universe-maker —for God.

The Wonder of Life

Another powerful argument for theism is the familiar but always mysterious force we call "life." There are a number of scientific theories about the origin of life. One is that seeds of life were carried to earth from outer space by meteors or cosmic dust. But this theory does not show how life itself originated. A more satisfying theory is that life started on earth by the accidental meeting of certain molecules. But neither of these theories, nor any other theories, explain what life is.

The science of biology has great achievements to its credit. It has discovered a great deal about how life functions. But no scientific theory has ever explained the essential quality of life—its purposive behavior. Wherever we find life, it is charged with purpose. We can see this in even the very lowest forms of life. For example, when an amoeba is hungry it reaches out for food, forms itself into new shapes and surrounds what it wants to eat. It acts with a purpose—to satisfy its hunger. This is the wonder that we cannot understand.

The basic unit of life is the organism—an amoeba, the whole dog or the whole man. And the organism is an organizing, purposive identity. A rock takes up space, but it does not organize the space it occupies. The rock could be smashed to pieces, and every fragment would be a complete new rock. But a broken dog is a dead dog; it has lost its life-giving, organizing power. It doesn't feed through the mouth. It doesn't wag its tail or lick its master's hand. And it is precisely this life-force that science cannot fathom.

The organization or design of life is very complex. Even the cell, the simplest form of organism, has the goal of sustaining its own life. In every phase of organic evolution, from the microbe to man, there is a fantastic degree of design and organization. We may not know if life serves a higher purpose, but we do know that every single bit of life is rich in its own purposes. It seems very difficult to explain life and its wonder without assuming a creator and designer—God.

The Wonder of Man

Besides the cosmic harmony and the purpose within living things, there is a third clue to the existence of God. Even those who find no need for God in understanding the universe and life may turn to God when they meet a quite different wonder—the wonder of man.

It has always been believed that man is radically different from other animals, and this difference—the factor that makes humanity human—has been the subject of speculation by philosophers, scientists and theologians for thousands of years. It is important, however, to see exactly where this difference lies. It used to be thought that only men could think, but careful study has proved that this was only a piece of human vanity. Chimpanzees are actually rather clever at getting bananas placed beyond their reach and have even used tools to help them in their efforts.

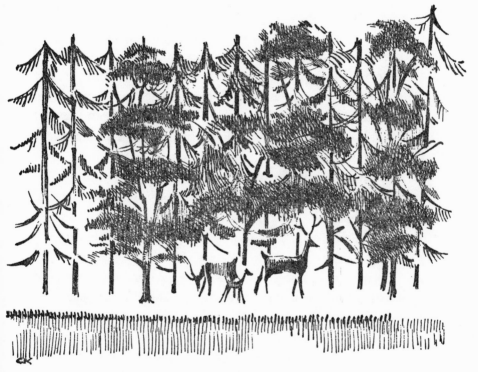

"In every phase of organic evolution, from the microbe to man, there is a fantastic degree of design and organization."

The chimpanzee using a stick to get his banana is doing the same kind of thinking as a man who uses a Geiger counter to unearth uranium deposits. Of course, the man is much smarter, but it's the same kind of smartness.

However, the brightest chimpanzee can only think about practical problems. And one of the things that makes a human being human is that he can think beyond the practical. He can think in terms of truth—not for any practical use, but truth for its own sake. Chimpanzees cannot do that.

This capacity cannot but make us marvel. Having evolved in the practical struggle for survival, on a planet on which every other animal struggles for survival, man has developed an even higher capacity—a holy curiosity, a desire to rise above his limited needs and to understand the world in which he lives. This capacity sets man apart from the animals. It manifests a non-animal element in him. This element we call spirit.

Man as an animal shares the natural instincts of other animals, but as a being endowed with spirit he has hopes and wants that make him different from the animals. One of these needs is the desire to seek the truth. Another is the urge to create and appreciate beauty.

Man is man because of his spirit. We see it in different ways at different times throughout man's history. The Greeks made major contributions to art, the Romans to law, the Germans and Italians to music and the English and Americans to technology. Perhaps more important than any of these is the Jewish contribution to moral consciousness including both individual and social justice.

It was the Jews who first believed that practicing love and justice was the right way to live and they devoted their lives to it. They believed in it as the noblest way to worship God. At a time when other people worshiped pagan idols, the Jews worshiped the moral force of a supernatural God.

So we see that the essence of man is a third wonder whose answer points in the direction of theism. When man evolved from the lower animals, as the scientific evidence indicates, then how did he acquire spirit, which is non-animal? Why should a creature exist who seeks for truth and beauty and the good? Remember, these are not "natural"; that is, we don't find them in nature except in man. The Bible's answer is that man was created in the image of God who is the source of truth, beauty and goodness.

Arguments Against Theism

We have given some powerful arguments for the theist's conviction that God exists. These arguments have been so convincing that they have been believed by the vast majority of all people who have ever lived.

There is no Indian tribe that has not worshiped gods. And all civilizations, from the time of the Egyptians and ancient Chinese to the present day, have been, not atheist or agnostic but theist.

But there have always been some men who did not believe or who doubted. Some of these have been great men. Usually they admit that the theist case is strong. But they insist that their case is better. And it must be admitted that they support it with some high-powered arguments.

The Problem of Disorder

One of these arguments is that the cosmic order is not perfect, as it should be if made by an all-powerful God. In all parts of the universe, along with the prevailing order, there are elements of disorder. In the heavens, stars sometimes explode or crash into each other. On earth, there are animals who live by preying on other animals. And man himself is subject to accident and disease.

The Problem of Evil

A second, even stronger argument against theism is the existence of evil, the bad things that are done by man. Evil is an ugly fact that we cannot escape. War is evil. Exploitation is evil. Dictatorship is evil. Crime is evil. Nowhere are any of the works of man entirely free from evil, and many thinkers have even insisted that all men are born evil. As Jews, we do not accept this extreme pessimism—but we still have to explain the existence of evil. Why should a God who is both good and all-powerful create evil? This question is, to say the least, very hard to answer. There are several theist answers, which we will consider in Chapter V. However, readers who know their Bible will already know some of them from the Book of Job and from the Book of Jeremiah.

The Atheist Position

The theist finds disorder and evil hard to explain. The atheist, on the other hand, can explain them without any difficulty. According to him, the world is the product of chance. There is nothing but matter and energy. He believes that whatever happens occurs by accident. So he does not have to explain disorder and evil.

It cannot be denied that the atheist can explain disorder and evil more easily than the theist. In fact, they are the most frequent causes for a person's becoming an atheist. When men make wars, it is easy to say, "If there is a God, why doesn't He stop this?"

But in spite of the strength of the atheist's answer to the problem of evil, his over-all position is essentially weak. The atheist sees only evil and disorder and overlooks or minimizes the great amounts of good and order. Most stars have continued in their courses for millions of years. Life has proceeded in an orderly evolution from simple one-celled organisms to the magnificent complexity of man. And even among men, there are more decent, law-abiding citizens than criminals, more heroes than cowards.

There is more good to explain than evil. No one can observe the sublime order of the universe unmoved, or feel the quickening of life without wonder, or respond to the human spirit without joy. It is very nearly impossible to ascribe these evidences of good to the workings of mathematical chance, yet the atheist must do just that.

The Agnostic Position

The agnostic's position is altogether different. He sees that the atheist cannot really say why there is cosmic order, life and human spirit. But he also sees that cosmic disorder and evil tremendously complicate the belief in God. He believes that the human mind has neither the evidence nor the capacity to choose between theism and atheism.

The agnostic must be taken seriously. Neither the case for theism nor atheism can be proved. Then why aren't we all agnostics? Why don't we all suspend judgment on the question of whether or not God exists? Since we don't know, why must we have an opinion? Why not honestly admit that the answer to the great question is beyond us?

Religion is Faith

The agnostic, as we have said, is very logical, but he forgets one thing which for the religious man is the most important thing of all—that religion is a commitment of the whole being, a way of life, *the* way of life. Religion is the deepest possible relation between man and God, a relation of love. As in purely human love, there is no room for mere opinion or half-heartedness. Either you love God or you don't. There is no middle way. Religion is not a way of thinking; it is a way of living. It makes no difference whether he who does not love God is an atheist or an agnostic. Emotionally—and religiously—the two are the same.

Every thinking man who is religious believes in God partly for the reasons given earlier in this chapter, but only partly. Reason can never be more than a small part of religious faith, because religion is primarily a matter of the heart.

According to Jewish tradition the highest good is love. Love is a total giving of the self, without question and without anxiety. For the atheist, his doubts are more important than believing. For the agnostic, his anxiety not to be wrong

30

is so great that he has lost all eagerness to be right; he cannot commit himself. But the religious man loves God passionately, and does not care that he cannot prove His existence with airtight logic. He feels with absolute sureness that a love so strong, so deep, must be answered.

The Bible breathes this certainty on every page. From the first word, it is written with loving faith in God's existence and His creative power. In the Psalms of David we have one of man's most glowing celebrations of religious faith, and David tells us that the essence of that faith is love, strength and inner peace.

Religious certainty does not come without effort and struggle. It is not to be reached by unaided thought or study. It has to be lived. The life of love, of faith, is the only road to that certainty. This is the way of life described by the Bible—the Jewish way of life.

If you have faith, as I do, that there is a God; if you believe that the wonder in the universe shows God's hand, the next question we must ask is: What is God like? Is He all-powerful? Is He one? Have people always recognized Him as one? Do we recognize Him as one today? What does the Jewish tradition teach us about these questions?

"... *Monotheism does not merely mean the bare assertion or belief that there is only one God. It also means the knowledge that God alone is absolute* .."

SH'MA *Yisrael Adonai Elohenu Adonai Echad.* Hear O Israel, the Lord our God, the Lord is One.

If you know only one of the many great statements of the Bible, it is a safe guess that this is the one. You probably know that it is in almost every religious service, that it is said at crucial points of the synagogue service, such as when the Torah is taken out of the ark. The pious Jew says it before he dies. We call it the "watchword of our faith," and that's exactly what it is. Next to the existence of God, the most important belief of Judaism is that God is one.

Religions that believe in one God are called *monotheistic,* and those that believe in many gods are called *polytheistic.* Judaism is probably the oldest monotheistic religion, but today all highly developed religions believe in one God. There are still some primitive tribes who worship trees and stones, but most civilized people who believe in God at all believe that He is invisible and that He is one.

The Problems of Polytheism

Polytheism is by its very nature unsatisfactory, and once its followers begin to reason things out they tend to become monotheists. The ancient Greeks, for example, believed in many gods and goddesses of love, war, wisdom, agriculture and so forth. But they soon realized that many gods might disagree with each other, fight among themselves and destroy the order of the universe. So they imagined that Zeus was the chief God and had power over all the others. Later they conceived the idea of a divine fate which ruled all the

35

gods, including Zeus. Thus, as the Greeks became more thoughtful, they became more monotheistic.

Today, few people believe in many gods. But the Sh'ma, which says that there is only one God, is still very important. For many people are polytheists without even knowing it.

Many people believe in God, but also believe that the universe is made of nothing but purposeless matter or energy. When they say the universe is independent of God, they make it God's equal; so they really believe in two gods.

There are other people who believe that God is merely the good in the universe. But they believe that there is evil in the universe as well, and that over this God has no power. Thus they make the power of evil into a second god. Their belief recalls the ancient Persian religion which believed in two ultimate powers, one good and the other evil, in eternal conflict with each other.

The Importance of Monotheism

But Judaism has always rejected the idea that God has no power over evil, and it has also rejected the idea that the universe is independent of God. Judaism has always said there is one God. The Sh'ma is the watchword of our faith. Why?

If we look a little more closely at the monotheism of the Bible and Jewish tradition, we soon discover that it means much more than the bare assertion that there is only one God. If you open your Bible at the Sh'ma passage (*Deuteronomy, Chapter VI, Verse 4ff.*) you will find that the next verse reads: "Thou shalt love the Lord thy God with all thy heart, all thy soul and all thy might." The fact that this statement follows the classical statement of monotheism proves that the Bible regards the two as essentially connected. And so they are. Biblical monotheism not only means that there is one God, it also means that we should follow and love Him with a heart that is one and undivided.

You are familiar with the story of the prophet Elijah contending with the priests of Ba'al on Mount Carmel (*1 Kings, Chapter 18, Verse 16ff.*). Perhaps you thought that they were arguing about who was the real God—Ba'al or the Lord of Israel? But Elijah's concern was quite different. What mattered to him was that you couldn't follow both Ba'al and the Lord of Israel. It had to be either one or the other. According to Elijah, a man could not really believe in God and yet follow Him with only part of his being. God demanded wholehearted devotion. And this is the core of monotheism in the Bible.

Now if we consider monotheism in this light, we see at once that we must fight for it today just as Elijah did in his day. For men are still polytheists in the sense that they follow many things, treating them as if they were gods. One man makes money his god, another glory and still another his nation. We may proclaim our belief in one God in synagogue, and our Christian neighbor may do the same in church. But most of us worship other things and thus, in effect, make gods out of them. And so we are all monotheists in theory and polytheists in practice.

Modern Forms of Idol Worship

This modern kind of polytheism is just as great an evil as the ancient polytheism. A person who treats as God that which is not God is worshiping idols. And perhaps most evils in human life result from just this. For example, there is nothing wrong with a person being eager to earn a living because he likes the things money can buy and because he wants security. But there is something very wrong with a person to whom money is the most important thing in life. The idea of money will drive charity out of such a person's heart and will eventually make his own life hateful to him.

There is nothing wrong with the desire to enjoy life, and, in fact, there cannot be a wholesome and good life without enjoyment. But it is quite wrong to make enjoyment the sole aim of life. It's like eating too much candy. After a while the candy doesn't taste good. A life of only pleasure has no meaning and is not enjoyed by the person who lives it.

To take yet another example, there is obviously nothing wrong with a person's being deeply attached to his work. This is a fine thing, and no one can be truly happy without liking his job. But it is wrong to make a god out of one's work. Consider a person who can never think of anything but his work, day or night. He stays in the office and never comes home. Such a person neglects himself as a human being. He also neglects his friends and his family. Finally he becomes a spiritually impoverished person; if his work suddenly stopped, he would find himself miserable, empty and devoid of purpose. It is one of the great tragedies of our time that today there are many such people.

38

Let us mention just one more example. Just as it is natural that we have a special love for our own family, it is natural that we have a special love for our own country. Therefore patriotism is a good thing. But there is something terribly wrong with *chauvinism*. A chauvinist is a person who thinks that his nation can do no wrong. Chauvinism leads to cruelty, tyranny and war. It is perhaps the greatest evil of our time.

"Chauvinism leads to cruelty, tyranny and war. It is perhaps the greatest evil of our time."

The Importance of Monotheism Today

We could give many more examples of modern idol worship, and in each case we would see that it is an evil. There are numerous things we human beings love, and which it is natural and good to love. But in many cases we are tempted to love excessively, to make an idol of what we love; and then this love at once becomes an evil.

Jewish monotheism teaches us that there is only one love which cannot be excessive; indeed a love which is adequate only if it is total and without qualifications. This is the love of God. Of course, it is not possible to love God at all unless one loves justice, charity and peace and—above all—one's fellow men.

We can sum up then by saying that monotheism does not merely mean the bare assertion or belief that there is only one God. It also means the knowledge that God alone is absolute, and that all the other "gods" we have in life are limited, and deserve only a limited loyalty. Even if we have this knowledge in theory, we are still continually tempted to ignore it in practice. We are continually tempted to give absolute loyalty to what has only limited value.

Only the person who has completely overcome this temptation can be called a monotheist in the full sense of the term. But perhaps nobody has ever fully overcome it. Monotheism represents an ideal toward which we must never stop struggling.

Chaptre Three: WHY DO WE BELIEVE
GOD CREATED THE WORLD?

If you believe, as I do, that God is one, our next question is, "Did God create the world?" Or did the world just happen? Did it take six days? Or six million years? Why is it hard to believe that God created the world? What does modern science think about this? What does Judaism teach us, and why?

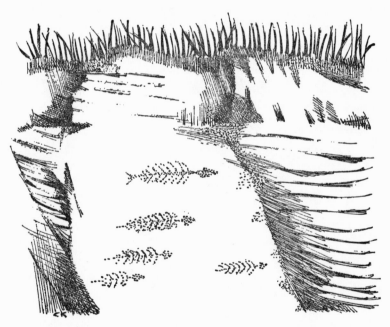

". . . But we now know that there was a period of thousands of years between monkeys and men, and millions of years before life appeared on the earth at all."

PERHAPS the most famous words of the whole Bible are those of its opening sentence, *In the beginning God created the heaven and the earth.* Even people who have only read a little of the Bible know those words and remember them. They are words that no Jew can ever forget, because they state one of Judaism's deepest beliefs, that God made the world.

This belief has always been a basic part of Jewish teaching. It is repeated throughout the Bible, especially by the prophets. It has been taught by the rabbis and scholars throughout our history. And Maimonides, the great Jewish thinker of the Middle Ages, wrote that it was next in importance to the belief in the oneness of God.

Almost everyone who believes in God believes that He created the world. In fact, as we have already shown in Chapter I, many people believe in God *because* they are convinced the universe must have a Creator. Otherwise they could not explain such phenomena as the cosmic order, life and the human spirit.

How Science Contradicts the Bible

But even though most theists believe that God created the world, many cannot accept the Jewish belief in creation as it is described in the Bible. The main reason for their rejection of the Bible's version of creation is its difference from the theories of modern science.

There are three areas of contradiction between the Biblical story and the scientific theories of creation. According

43

to the Bible, this is the order in which the world was created: Heaven and earth, light, day and night, the dry land and water, plants, stars, sun and moon, animals and, finally, man. This list does not agree with today's scientific knowledge. And the Bible says the world was created in six days, but we now know that there was a period of thousands of years between monkeys and men, and millions of years before life appeared on the earth at all. Finally, the Bible says that each kind of animal was created separately, by a special act of God. Science, of course, tells us that the higher animals, including man, evolved from the lower animals.

Some People Fear the Truth

These three contradictions are so serious that they may seem to make it impossible for a thinking person to believe that the Bible and science are both true. And history is full of people afraid of the truth who have tried to suppress scientific discoveries because they conflicted with religious beliefs. This happened when the Inquisition made Galileo renounce the theory that the earth revolved around the sun.

It also happened more recently in Tennessee. In 1925 it was against the law to teach evolution in Tennessee. A teacher named Scopes broke the law and was brought to trial. Both sides were argued by brilliant lawyers, and the trial created a sensation that is still remembered. William Jennings Bryan, speaking for the prosecution, argued passionately in defense of the fundamentalist position in religion; but his opponent, Clarence Darrow, easily made him look ridiculous.

There is a valuable lesson to be learned from the Scopes trial. No matter how much religion and science disagree, we can be sure that the people who try to suppress scientific progress are not acting wisely. Some of those who have done this in the past may have had good intentions, but they were certainly misguided. No religion which is worth believing in can possibly be helped by the suppression of truth.

Since a well-informed Jew, like any other educated person, must accept the theory of evolution as a proven fact, how can he believe that the world was created by God? Certainly it is true that the evidence contradicts the Biblical story of creation.

Science Wants to Know How

But if we read the Bible more carefully, we soon find that it is not really interested in scientific theories. It is looking at the world in an entirely different way, and it is looking for different things. Science is looking for causes, dates, measurements. Science wants to know when the world originated. Exactly how? How long did it take? In what order did the various parts of the world come into being?

But the Bible is not interested in these things. It mentions some of them, but it never talks about them for more than a few words. Others it does not mention at all. For instance, the Bible starts, "In the beginning God created..." But when was the beginning? We are not told. On the other hand, we are told that the world was created in six days. This sounds very exact. But what does the Bible mean here by the phrase, "six days"? Even the Midrash, a very orthodox book, which often takes the Bible literally, implies that these "six days" need not be taken literally; it can just as well mean six thousand years, or six million years. After all, how would you count "days" before there was the day and the night? The subject of most interest to science is *how* the world was created. And it is precisely on this subject that the Bible is completely silent. It tells us that God made the world, and for the Bible that is enough. It does not tell us the *how* of creation.

Religion Wants to Know Why

If the Bible is not interested in these things, what is it interested in? The answer is that the Bible is concerned with questions outside the scope of science. It is interested in just those questions that science cannot answer. Science wants to know how things happen; the Bible wants to know *why*.

The Bible wants to show us the meaning of things. And the meaning behind the story of creation is in the order of creation. It is told for the purpose of emphasizing the importance of God's last and most perfect creation—man.

Science is the study of causes and effects. When it discovers that heat causes water to boil, it then tries to find out what causes heat. It is always pushing back, looking for the next cause. But religion is not particularly interested in this cause and that cause. What it wants to know more than anything else is the ultimate cause of everything. It wants to know the beginning of the entire universe, and it wants to make sure that the universe has a beginning. Above all, it wants to know that its beginning is from God. Science is not concerned with this greatest of all questions, because no matter how far back it pushes its investigations, science can never come to the very first thing that ever happened, to the beginning of everything. Because whenever science carries its explorations beyond a certain point, it always comes up against the big unsolvable mysteries—the mysteries of cosmic order, life and the human spirit.

Why We Believe That God Created the World

It is just these deepest mysteries of all, the ones forever beyond the reach of science, that are religion's concern. Religion does not ask how the world came into being. It leaves that question to science. But religion is deeply concerned with the ultimate origin and meaning of the world. Its answer is that the world comes from God—and that God made the world so that He could create goodness. In the first verses of Genesis, at the end of every day, God looks at what He has made and sees that it is good. And at the end of the sixth and last day of creation, after God has made Adam and Eve, the Bible gives us its most important message, *And God saw everything that He had made, and, behold, it was very good.*

It may seem obvious to you that the universe is good, because this is the view generally accepted in America today. But in the ancient world, except in Israel, it was the minority view. Many wise men believed that existence is evil, or at best, neither good nor evil; and there are still philosophers today who think in this way. For example, many Greek philosophers believed that it is better to die

47

than to live, and better still not to have been born. The Buddhist religion still teaches a similar doctrine.

Throughout the Bible there is a strongly optimistic view of the universe. And this view has been the one held by nearly all Jewish sages at nearly all times.

From what we have shown about the different goals of religion and science, it follows that the contradictions between the Bible and the theory of evolution are not really contradictions at all. The Bible and science cannot contradict each other, because they are not talking about the same thing. The Bible seems to contradict the theory of evolution only when its words are taken literally. And not even the most Orthodox Jews accept a completely literal interpretation of the Bible. When the Bible describes the creation of the world, it is not presenting a primitive and out-of-date scientific theory. It is giving us a religious message in symbols and pictures. And the real meaning of these symbols and pictures is that the world is good, because God made it. Judaism contradicts only those who say the world is evil or meaningless. It does not contradict science, since on questions of ultimate meaning, science has nothing to say.

God's World Is a Good World

The belief in creation is the faith that the world comes from God and that therefore, the world is good. This belief, of course, has a great deal to do with how we live our lives right now.

In ancient times there were devil-worshiping religions which believed that the world was created, at least partly,

48

by an evil power. And there were many philosophers who believed that the world was produced by chance.

Even today there are people who believe that the world "just happened," through an accidental coming together of atoms. These people are often good, honest and intelligent,

"In fact, Judaism has frequently been attacked because its uncompromising optimism seems to overlook the tremendous amount of evil and disorder in the world."

LIBRARY — LUTHERAN SCHOOL
OF THEOLOGY AT CHICAGO

PATHS TO JEWISH BELIEF

but they are helpless victims of their pessimistic philosophy. They are convinced that the world is meaningless or maybe even evil. As a result, they are usually cynical or desperate. At best, they look for meaning and goodness inside themselves alone, and have to withdraw from the outside world. Many pious hermits have been such people, depressed by their feeling that the world is a wicked place.

But there have been very few Jewish hermits, because Judaism has always fought against such attitudes. It has always asserted against them its firm faith that the world is good because God created it. In fact, Judaism has frequently been attacked because its uncompromising optimism seems to overlook the tremendous amount of evil and disorder in the world. Naturally, Judaism has always been aware of evil and disorder and there are several traditional Jewish solutions to this terrible problem. We will deal with these solutions in a later chapter (Chapter V). But every Jewish explanation of evil has always considered it as part of an essentially good world created by a good God. Maimonides spoke for the modern Jew as well as the ancient Jew when he said, "Creation is a belief next in importance to the belief in divine unity."

Chapter Four: HOW DO WE
PICTURE GOD IN OUR MIND?

Did God create the world with hands? Did He see the world with eyes when He said it was good? Does He hear our prayers with ears? When we do something good, does He know it in His mind? What does God look like? How do we picture God? Why does the Bible talk of God as having an "outstretched arm"? Why does the Bible tell of the "voice of God"?

"Judaism is based on the relation between man and an understanding, loving, answering God."

VERY young children often imagine God as an old man with a long white beard. When we grow older, we smile at this idea as a childish fancy. We know that He is not an old man with a white beard. But if He is not this, then what is He?

This is one of the hardest of all questions, and it may even be impossible to answer.

The Nature of God Is Unknowable

The Bible teaches us that God is infinite and invisible, and therefore forbids the making of any likeness of God. No synagogue or temple contains His picture. However, we cannot help thinking about God and forming mental images of Him. But we must always remember that these images are made by us and are therefore only human creations. Nothing we can possibly imagine can resemble God, who made us. It is impossible for us to picture God as He must be.

But because we are human, we always think of God in human terms. Because of our human limitations, our thought about God must always be anthropomorphic—that is, it must endow God with human characteristics He doesn't really have. Even when we think of God as a super-person we are still thinking of Him in human terms.

It is not enough to imagine God as a man. And it is not even enough to imagine Him as a super-man.

Can we then imagine Him as an impersonal force or substance which fills the whole universe? This is an attractive idea to scientifically minded people, because they are familiar with the forces of electricity, magnetism and gravity.

But there is something terribly inadequate about the idea of an impersonal God. If God is an impersonal force, how can we pray to Him? How can we say to Him, *Baruch Ata Adonai*, Praised be Thou, O Lord? And this is the beginning of nearly every Jewish blessing that we address to God.

Judaism is based on the relation between man and an understanding, loving, answering God. In every Jewish prayer God is addressed as "You" or "Thou," or referred to as "He." But you cannot use these "personal pronouns" for an impersonal force or substance. You may have gotten angry at a chair you knocked against and said, "You stupid chair!" as though the chair knocked against you. But you didn't really think the chair was stupid—or intelligent. And you knew that it couldn't listen to you—that it wasn't really a "you." After you calm down, you always feel a little silly for having talked that way to an inanimate object.

Prayer can only have meaning, then, if addressed to a God who is more than a force or substance. When we say "You" or "Thou" to God, we must be sure He understands and responds, or at least is able to understand and respond. Otherwise, prayer would be the same as talking to yourself. We may not know how God responds to our prayers, but that is not so terribly important. The most important thing in prayer is that God does or at least can respond to us. To pray to a force that cannot hear is no better than to worship idols or to speak to wood and stone.

We Talk to God and God Hears Us

Religion is the belief in a living connection between man and God. It is the way of life of men who feel the presence

54

of God and communicate with Him through prayer. Prayer is a kind of intimate conversation or talking, and we can only talk meaningfully to other persons. So a religion based on prayer must picture God as a person. So again we find ourselves thinking of God as a person. And in a way, this is better.

God surely resembles a human person far more closely than He does an impersonal force. Such forces may be so vast as to have us wholly at their mercy. Still, there is a sense in which the weakest and humblest human person is superior to all the cosmic forces taken together. He can know truth, do good, feel beauty and religious awe, while they can do nothing of the kind. For he has a mind and they are mindless. But can we think of God as mindless? If we do, we think of God as less perfect even than we are! But He must surely exceed us infinitely in perfection.

So if we must choose between picturing God as an impersonal force or as a person, it is better to picture Him as a person. That picture too is inadequate, of course, for God is infinite, but it is the best picture we can form.

But why have a picture of God at all? Why not admit once and for all that God is unknowable? Is that what the Bible is telling us when it forbids the making of images and pictures?

Even the Bible Pictures God

No, not exactly. For the Bible itself, even though it insists that God is unknowable, is full of all kinds of images of Him. It describes Him as speaking and commanding and stretching forth His arm. The Bible does not mean that God

55

has a voice and eyes and arms, or even a mind or a heart in any way like our own. Then why does it talk of God in these human terms? There must be a good reason why the Bible so often uses this figurative way of speaking.

The answer to the question is this: God is not just a distant reality which never enters our lives; we can experience His

"And that experience is closer to loving contact with another person than it is to any other feeling."

presence in our hearts. But where the heart feels, the mind must picture and the lips must speak. This is why for the Bible, and for us as well, it is necessary to form pictures of God, even though we know that the noblest picture we can form is still inadequate.

The most exalted picture we can make of God is as a person. Strictly speaking, He is not a person, because He is so much more than anything or anyone we know by that word. But personality comes closer than any other human concept to the true nature of God. We know this, because though we cannot know God we can experience Him. And that experience is closer to loving contact with another person than it is to any other feeling. The heart of religion lies in this experience. When we say "Praised art Thou, O Lord," we do not mean the word "Thou" literally, but it is the best way we can express our belief that God is present with us and does not forsake us.

Chapter Five: WHY DOES GOD
PERMIT EVIL?

We have pictured a God whom we can talk to, a God who answers our prayers. We have faith that He hears us. We have faith that He wants the world to be good. Then why does He permit evil in the world? Why does He permit a tooth to hurt, a baby to starve, a man to die? Why does He allow cheating, bribery, killing, every kind of wickedness? And for what reason do innocent people suffer?

". . . We must never forget that the evils of human history often assume monstrous proportions."

EVERY one of the higher religions thinks of God as all-powerful. It's true that some primitive tribes believe that their gods can get sick and die, but such ideas are unknown among civilized people. The God of all the historic monotheistic religions is above such limitations. He cannot be God unless He is all-powerful. Nevertheless there have always been thoughtful people who denied the omnipotence of God.

The ancient Persians believed in a being almost as powerful as God, who worked against God and limited His power. There are even modern philosophers who believe that God's powers are limited—including such great men as Bergson, A. N. Whitehead and the American, William James. But a limited God is not the God of the Jewish people.

It is important for us to find out why these thinkers believed in a limited God. For if they were right, then Judaism must be wrong.

Judaism Believes in an All-Powerful God

Judaism has always stressed the omnipotence of God, because only a good and all-powerful God can make us certain that the world ultimately is good, even at times when it doesn't seem good. The believing Jew trusts in God at all times, and he never accepts any philosophy that puts limitation on God's power. In the Bible, the prophet Isaiah defended strict monotheism against the Persian belief in two powers. And Maimonides and other medieval Jewish philosophers argued against the Greeks' view that God did not create matter. Instead they agreed with the Book of Genesis that God created the world out of nothing.

The Great Problem of Evil

But if God made the world and everything in it, He must have made evil too. And this is our great problem.

In this chapter we are not going to solve the problem of evil. What we will see is whether the presence of evil rules out the goodness and the omnipotence of God.

Some religions try to hide from this terrible question by denying the existence of evil. But evil will not let itself be denied. We can always find it.

There is not a single human being who has not experienced evil at first hand; wherever we turn, we can find it. Who has never been sick? And who does not know a friend or relative who died? Even if we could imagine a person who had never spent an unhappy hour all his life, he would eventually have to die.

Besides these physical evils, we are all familiar with moral evil, which is still worse. Antisemitism and racial and religious hatreds are moral evils. And whenever we think of men like Hitler, we know how terrible moral evil can be.

Atheists and agnostics may suffer from evil and fight against it as much as anyone. But at least they have no difficulty in explaining it. For them, it is a natural part of the universe, since the universe, as they see it, was formed by chance and is without purpose. So they say, "Why shouldn't it be evil as well as good?"

But the theist faces the opposite problem, the big problem. If the universe is created by a good and all-powerful God, why does He create evil, or at least permit evil to exist? This is what the Book of Job is concerned with, and what the prophet Jeremiah meant when he cried out, "Wherefore doth the way of the wicked prosper?"

It seems natural to believe that a good God could create only a good world. Therefore many thoughtful people decided that God's power was limited because He had not made the world completely good. This idea explains evil—but it takes away from God that power that makes Him truly God. If He is powerless to avoid evil, then we cannot look to Him for help and comfort when evil befalls us. But it is just then that we need God most.

We need Him to give us the assurance that even in the midst of evil we are not forsaken by Him, that we are not the victims of blind chance.

If we tried to sum up, in a single word, the secret of Jewish strength through the ages, that word would be the Hebrew word *Davkah*—"nevertheless." In times of greatest tragedy the Jew adhered, "nevertheless," most stubbornly to his faith. But how could he have done so unless he had believed that God was both all-powerful and good—that God was in control of the evil things that happen to us as well as of the good?

Is Evil Always Bad?

We know we won't be able to solve the problem of evil in this book. After all, it has remained unsolved for thousands of years. But we hope to be able to make the problem a little clearer and perhaps come a little nearer to a solution.

In the first place, we must ask if what seems to be evil is always really evil.

Take the example of pain. Nobody denies that a toothache is an evil thing. But if our teeth didn't hurt when cavities formed, we wouldn't know when to go to the dentist, and the sickness might spread. In a toothache, as in most other physical aches, the pain seems to be a signal that something is wrong. And if we pay attention to the signal, we can restore ourselves to health. The signal hurts, but it has to hurt to make us take notice. Ultimately, this kind of pain is good.

But this leads us to another question: Why does God let us get sick? No matter how many brilliant discoveries medicine makes, sickness is always with us. And even if one day the doctors learn how to cure all diseases, they will never prevent old age and death. Everything that is born must one day die. Therefore our ultimate question is, Why does God allow death?

Is Death Really Evil?

Try to imagine a world in which no living thing ever dies. Plants and animals and people would keep coming into the world, but no one would ever leave. Soon the earth would be terribly crowded. The world would be as packed as the New York subway during rush hour.

There wouldn't be enough food to go around, and all our time would be spent in the search for something to eat. When we found it, we would have to fight to keep it. All the other people and animals would be trying to get it, too.

Of course, you can try to imagine a better world in which there would be enough food, drink and shelter for everyone. There would be no fighting, and we would all be friends. But no matter how big you made such a world, if living things multiplied endlessly, the day would come when the struggle for food and elbowroom would start all over again. Only a world that kept growing with the population could keep from getting crowded, and such a world is almost impossible to imagine.

You might then try to imagine a world without either birth or death. Then all creatures could live together in peace, harmony and plenty. But the catch is that life as we know it means being born and growing and dying. What makes living organisms different from inorganic matter is that they develop and mature.

This life, as we know it, finds beauty, purpose and adventure only by growing. And without growth and change there would be eternal boredom, which is closer to death than to life.

Coming back to the problem of evil, we can say that some apparent evils are a kind of detour to good. Physical pain is often a warning which helps us steer clear of sickness, and even death appears to be a necessary part of the world as we know it. True, we could imagine a world wholly without evil, and this would be entirely different from the one in which we live. In fact, the Bible does just this when forming the picture of the garden of Eden, in which there was neither pain nor death. But the Bible also tells us that we are no longer in the garden of Eden, and that the world is still

65

under divine providence. Thus it believes that the physical evils of our world sometimes serve a good purpose which may be clear to mortal man.

And so our Jewish heritage tells us that we must first abolish physical evil whenever we can. When we cannot destroy it, we must fight it to the best of our ability. Second, if we can neither abolish nor control a particular evil, we should look for a hidden good in it. And finally, if we cannot imagine what good end some apparent evils serve, we must always remember that God works in ways we cannot fully understand.

How Bad Are Moral Evils?

So far we have only talked about physical evils, such as pain, disease and death. These are natural enemies of man that he always fights against. But now we must deal with the moral evils which man himself creates. These evils—including cruelty, oppression, hatred and prejudice—are terribly familiar to all of us. There can be no necessity for man to perpetrate these evils, yet man always has.

Moral evil is a much harder problem to solve than physical evil. We have seen that pain, and even death, may be necessary parts of life. But what good purpose can possibly be served by envy, cruelty, injustice, oppression, and callousness?

There is absolutely no good purpose that we can ever find in a moral evil. When we call it a moral evil we mean just that. We mean that in the sight of God it is wrong, that it is against God's will and against His laws which He laid down for men so that they could live together in peace.

66

If a man dies, that is a physical evil, and we can learn to accept it. But if a man deliberately kills another man for greed or envy, this is moral evil. It never has a good purpose and it is always wrong. It can never be a means to a hidden good. Moral evil is something that men do that is contrary to the will of God.

Why does an all-powerful and good God allow this?

"Yet Job said: 'Even though He slay me yet will I trust in Him'."

We can't possibly believe that God *wants* us to do evil. The Torah specifically bids us do good rather than evil, and the prophets look forward to a messianic future when moral evil will have ceased. So moral evil can't be a means to a hidden good brought about by God.

Why God Permits Moral Evil

According to the Bible story, when God first made Adam and Eve, they were innocent, and guilty of no evil. Then why did God permit mankind to fall into such terrible ways when they left the Garden of Eden? Since then, men have done much harm to one another. Soon it may even be possible for men to destroy the entire earth, and we know that it is not inconceivable that they might actually do it.

The Book of Genesis *(Chapters 3 and 4)* states the position of Judaism: Man, not God, is responsible for moral evil. God created man, but He endowed him with a free will. This free will was one of God's greatest gifts to man, and God meant him to make good use of it. But God would not force man to be good. If He did, then man's will would not be free. So when Adam first chose evil instead of good, it was his action, not God's—and when man today continues to choose evil, it is still his action and not God's.

There is nothing here that contradicts the idea of divine omnipotence. God is able to prevent man from choosing evil, but He does not do this. Thus, man can create evil because God permits him to do so for a higher good. That higher good, according to Judaism, is human freedom.

Let us compare God to a teacher and mankind to His

pupils. As you have probably observed, there are two basic methods of teaching. The first method is the way we are all taught our ABC's. The teacher makes us say the same things over and over again, until we remember them. This is a good method for teaching simple facts and dates. But it doesn't work when we are trying to master a difficult subject. Then a good teacher must use the second method, which is to make the pupil think for himself.

The first method is efficient and, if the teacher knows his subject, the pupil's answers are always right. But though he knows everything, he may understand nothing. His knowledge is like that of a calculating machine, and his mind is not free.

If the teacher wants to cultivate a free mind, he must use the second method. He must let the pupil find things out for himself. This method too is efficient, and it produces pupils who think for themselves. Of course, if you think for yourself, there is the danger you may often come up with the wrong answers, as Adam did.

This is a dilemma which your parents had to face, particularly when you were very young. Your parents wanted to protect you from errors and dangers that they understood but which you may not have known about. And, on the other hand, they wanted you to grow up self-reliant, and able to make your own decisions, including your own mistakes. Many of the things you learned, you learned by experience, and you will learn many other things in the same way. So part of the problem of being a parent is to find the right blend of freedom and authority in bringing up a child who is protected, but not over-protected; free, but not without discipline; yet able to make his own decisions.

When God created man, He faced the same problem. He could have willed man to be good. But he permitted man to do moral evil, because only in this way could He give man his noblest gift, the human freedom of choice. Man can be a criminal, but he can also be a saint.

You must not think for a moment that we have now solved the problem of evil. We have explained why evil exists, but we cannot accept it. For we must never forget that the evils of human history often assume monstrous proportions. And when we think of such things as concentration camps or slavery or atomic bombs, we cannot help wondering if it might not have been better, after all, had man been a dumb animal without free will. But then we remember the good and the great goodness that man can achieve. And we know that with all our courage we must fight against evil.

Why Must the Innocent Suffer?

We have explained why there is physical evil, and why God allows moral evil. But what is most difficult to understand—most difficult of all—is that the evil done by the wicked is too often suffered by the innocent. How can a just and merciful God permit innocent people to become the victims of murderers, tyrants and persecutors? How can He permit innocent children to die in a war?

This question, which is the real heart of the whole problem of evil, has tormented religious people from the times of Job and Jeremiah till today. Often this kind of evil is so terrible that we cannot imagine any kind of purpose behind it, human or divine. Why has God so often allowed some men to enslave others, depriving them of their God-given freedom? What reason can be found for mass slaughter of innocent people?

Questions such as these nobody can ever answer, and the Book of Job teaches us that it is wrong even to try. We can sympathize with the suffering of the innocent; but we can never understand it.

But the Book of Job also teaches us that, though men don't know and can't know the purpose of this kind of evil, it may yet have a purpose—known only to God. Job himself is the greatest example of all times of this saving trust. He was a good man who suffered the worst misfortunes a man can suffer, and neither he nor anyone else knew why. Yet Job said: "Even though He slay me yet will I trust in Him." (*Chapter 13, verse 15*). It was this belief, it was this faith, it was this trust in the goodness of God, that allowed Job to survive.

PART TWO

MAN

"Man is but little lower than the angels." What does this mean? Is man different from the animals? How is he different from the animals? Is the difference true of all men or of only a few men? Why does Judaism insist on equal opportunity for all men? Why does Judaism say that all men are equal in the sight of God?

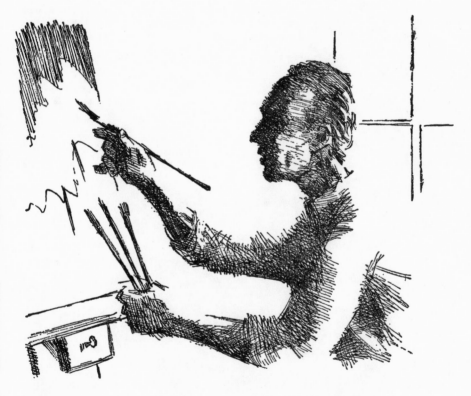

"Only man can consciously create and enjoy beauty."

THE RELATIONSHIP between God and man is the chief concern of most religions. To know what this relationship ought to be, we have to know as much as we can about man. What Judaism says about man is in one simple sentence in the Bible: *God created man in His own image.*

If you look again at Chapter I, you will see that we have already discussed what these words mean about the nature of man. As the image of God, man is different from all other animals. In fact, he is the crown of creation.

We examined the evidence and found that the difference between man and the animals is not physical. There are physical differences, of course, but they are not so important. The big difference is not emotional, either. We all know that dogs can be jealous or sad or happy. We finally found some very significant spiritual differences between man and the animals, such as man's desire to search for truth and goodness.

These wants make man unique because they are not useful and they don't serve the purpose of self-preservation. Animals act to provide themselves and their young with food, drink and shelter, and they think for the same purposes.

But men do not seek truth only as a help in the struggle for survival. They also seek truth for its own sake. And at their best men do what is good, not because they hope to gain by it, but because they feel a sense of justice or brotherly love.

Man Loves Beauty

Another kind of spiritual activity that sets man apart from the animals is artistic creativity. Man is not the only being that is creative. Birds build nests and sing songs, and beavers build dams. Some animal creations, such as beehives and ant hills, show a great deal of skill in their construction. But they are very different from human creations because they are always made exclusively to serve a useful purpose.

Human beings make many objects for useful purposes, but we also aim at something else—beauty. No matter how large and comfortable a house may be, it doesn't please us unless we like its looks. And even automobiles are judged partly by the grace of their lines and the pleasantness of their colors.

Human creations often have no use at all, and are made for no other purpose than to express beauty. Poems, paintings and symphonies have no value in the struggle for existence. It is true that sometimes artists make money or become famous, but no real artist does creative work only for these reasons. A good painting would be beautiful whether or not the artist was paid for his work. And, in the same spirit, anyone who truly appreciates a song or a poem, is not just relaxing or being entertained. He is experiencing a unique kind of enjoyment, the enjoyment of beauty.

Only man can consciously create and enjoy beauty. And this ability, which we call the *esthetic faculty*, is shared by all men and by every civilization. Different cultures produce different kinds of art, but all forms of art are based on universal human feelings. Recently some explorers in the jungles of South America made an interesting experiment. They played a phonograph recording of a Mozart work for a tribe of primitive Indians who had never heard European music. The Indians were deeply moved. And if you have ever heard a record of primitive Indian or African music, you know that we find it strange—but beautiful.

Man's Hunger for Religion

There is still another spiritual capacity into which all the others somehow enter—the sense of religious awe and devotion. The earliest records of man show that he has always worshiped a force greater than himself or anything else in the natural world. At first, he located this force in trees or fire or even man made objects. But his worship was always directed at a divine force behind the trees and fire, never at the things themselves. The earliest religion was superstitious and idolatrous, but it was genuine because it grew out of a search for truth, goodness and beauty, mingled with religious awe.

So you see that even the most ignorant and primitive form of religion separates man from the beasts. Because animals are never sinners, and they are never idolators. Only man can be these things.

This special sense of religion, these special capacities for goodness, truth and beauty, are not just for a few men, but all men. They are not the obligations of a few, but all. The Bible stresses this universality in the story of the creation of Adam.

Adam Is Everyone's Father

When the Bible says that all mankind is descended from the same original father, it is not propounding a scientific theory about the origin of man; it is saying something about our life here and now. A Talmudic rabbi interpreted the Bible's meaning for us in these words: "Why did God create only one man? So that no man can say, 'My descent is nobler than yours!' "

However, as we know, many people have refused to accept the idea of equality. They argue that human beings are obviously unequal. For instance, Einstein was more intelligent than most people, and Rembrandt more talented. The prophet Amos was surely superior in moral vision to a gangster. The enemies of democracy conclude that what is true for individuals is true for races and nations, and that some are better than others.

This argument sounds good—until you give it a little thought. If you think about it, it would not be fair to call a man stupid if he never had an opportunity to study and learn. And if the gangster had not been brought up in a miserable slum, it is altogether possible that he might have become an able and respected citizen.

If it is difficult to compare individuals, it is impossible to compare whole races. No two races or nations have ever had the same history and the same opportunities. The Negroes have never had the opportunities of white Americans. Therefore we cannot say that they are inferior in any way.

But all this is not really quite the point. The point is not whether all people have the same talents or the same amount

"*The Negroes have never had the opportunities of white Americans. Therefore we cannot say that they are inferior in any way.*"

of intelligence. It is whether they have the same rights—the right to the same opportunity to develop their God-given spirituality, which consists of the urge toward truth, goodness, beauty and the worship of God. All these impulses have one thing in common. They are a part of human freedom. They must be developed from within. Every man has this capacity for self-development, and this is just what the Bible means when it says that man was created in the image of God. To deny or to lessen this capacity in some men is an offense against the divine image.

God Wants Us to Choose Good

These spiritual capacities can only be realized in a man who acts because he wants to do something, rather than because he is compelled to do it. You can be forced to go to school, but you cannot be compelled to become wise. No one can make you use your intelligence. Nor are you really good if you refrain from evil only because you are afraid of your parents or society. True goodness can only come from your own will to be good. And the same thing is true of artistic creation and religious feeling.

Undoubtedly, the knowledge, goodness, esthetic sense and religious piety of some people are more highly developed than those of others. But no matter how great or small your capacities are, in these fields you are always on your own. You can learn from others, but only by making what you learn part of your own understanding.

Therefore each man has the right, as well as the duty, to realize his spiritual possibilities. And no one besides himself can take the responsibility for his spiritual development. That is the ultimate reason why every man has the right to be free, and why a just society must treat all men equally.

Now we are in a position to understand fully why man is the crown of creation and why all men are entitled to equal rights. Only a man—not an animal—can know truth, do good, create beauty and worship God. But, too, only a man can speak lies, do evil, pervert beauty into ugliness and commit idolatry. At his highest, man rises far above the animals. At his lowest, he sinks far below them.

This shows that man as the crown of creation is in a position which is dangerous as well as challenging. We can sink into deepest depravity; but we can also rise to a position "but little lower than the angels." This is what the Torah means when it says that God has placed both good and evil before us, between which we must choose. But God wants us to choose good.

The Bible also tells us that no one ever seems wholly to choose good. Even Moses was not free from sin. But this can be no excuse for us to cease struggling toward truth, goodness, beauty and piety. Rabbi Tarphon in the *Sayings of the Fathers* said, "It is not thy duty to complete the work, but neither art thou free to desist from it."

Chapter Seven: HOW RIGHT IS RIGHT?
HOW WRONG IS WRONG?
CAN WE CHOOSE BETWEEN THEM?

Man needs truth and beauty, but he also needs something else. Man needs to be good. But how do we know what is good? Is good always good in the same way? Is something that was right for our ancestors right for us today? Does God force us to be good? Or do we ourselves choose the right way? What does Judaism tell us? Is the Jewish way the only way? What are other good ways? What do we mean by moral insight?

"According to Jewish tradition,
God made such a covenant with the people of Israel."

THE STUDY of the right behavior of man toward other men is called ethics. In Judaism, ethics is an inseparable part of religion, because you cannot establish a right relationship with God if you do not establish at the same time a right relationship with your fellow men. Therefore we can describe Judaism as an ethical religion.

Ethics is concerned with such matters as justice, charity, brotherly love and peace. Jewish teaching has a great deal to say about these virtues, and if we are to live in accordance with the Jewish tradition, we must practice them every day.

You are probably deeply impressed by the ethics of the prophets and by the Ten Commandments. And you try to live by them just as Jews have tried to live by them for many years.

But how do we know what is really good? How do we know these ideas are right? You know that these ideas are thousands of years old. Is it certain that after all this time they are still valid?

Can We Choose Between Right and Wrong?

So our question at this point is whether we ever know what is right or wrong. But there is still another question we must ask. Even if we know what is right or wrong, does this help us any? Can our knowledge of right and wrong affect our actions? Have we the ability to choose between good and evil? Or are our actions due to causes beyond our control?

According to some people, we think and act as we have been trained by our environment, following the impulses with which we were born. These people believe we have no choice.

If it is really true that we have no freedom of choice, then we aren't responsible for what we do. We cannot blame anyone for being a criminal, or praise anyone for being a saint. We are merely the slaves of heredity or environment, or of a mixture of both.

This view sounds quite persuasive, and it is even supported by some religions. As you may know, there are several religions that believe an all-powerful God controls the human will as well as nature. They believe an iron necessity governs the world, and that man can only accept it and submit to it; that he cannot change it. These religions are called *fatalistic* because they believe that everything is decided by fate. A modern scientific version of fatalism is called *determinism*.

But Judaism rejects fatalism and determinism. We can see how important free will is in Judaism by contrasting the Jewish and Greek ideas about prophecy. In an ancient Greek legend, the prophetess Cassandra knew that her native city of Troy was doomed to be destroyed by the Greeks. She walked through the streets of Troy, crying out her prophecy, but no one paid any attention. Soon the city was destroyed. Even though Cassandra had correct knowledge of the future and the will to change it, she was helpless. Those ancient Greeks who believed in fate thought that nothing anybody knew or did could change the course of events.

How different is the Biblical story of Jonah! He also prophesied the doom of a great city. But in his case, the inhabitants of the city listened to Jonah, repented of their sins, and the city was saved.

You can easily see that in Jewish tradition prophecy does not mean the prediction of a future that cannot be avoided. On the contrary, as this example shows, the Jewish prophets pointed to a future that threatened—only if the people did not change their ways. But the whole point of prophesying was to get the people to change. Here, as elsewhere, Judaism is a religion of human freedom.

A Covenant Means the Responsibility to Choose

Rather than regarding God as blind fate, and man as a mere plaything of fate, Judaism sees God and man as partners and co-workers. This is expressed in the idea of a covenant, a *b'rith*. A covenant is a relationship in which two parties freely accept certain obligations toward each other. According to Jewish tradition, God made such a covenant with the people of Israel. He also made a covenant with the entire human race, in which humanity promised to live by the moral law.

Though it is probably impossible to prove the reality of free will, there are some very good reasons why Judaism insists on this doctrine as a truth accepted on faith, by anyone who is serious about his moral responsibilities. One of these reasons is obvious. If you believe that everything is going to happen the same way, regardless of what you do about it, you are very likely to do nothing at all. You tend to become extremely passive and irresponsible. For example, Cain is quoted in the Midrash as saying, "If fate has made me a murderer, it is not my fault." But, of course, it was Cain's fault. Cain, not fate, killed Abel.

Why do you suppose that you are not in jail? Is it because your parents brought you up well? But what about your parents? Why aren't they criminals? Is it because their parents brought them up well? If you carry this kind of reasoning to its logical conclusion, you'll eventually come to a dead end. And you'll never be able to find out how civilization and morality started.

Thousands of years ago, people were savages without ethical standards. Naturally, they could teach their children only what they themselves knew. It is impossible to account for the progress of history unless we assume that, somewhere along the line, certain individuals made free, creative contributions of their own. These individuals could not have been mere products of their parents' upbringing. And once you admit that some people have this freedom, you must admit that everyone has it, though some may use it more productively than others.

It is true that environment and heredity are tremendously powerful forces. But the freedom of the individual is an even stronger force. Someone coming from a bad environment has two strikes against him, and someone coming from a good environment has all the breaks on his side. But nothing forces the one to become a criminal or the other a saint.

It is safe to assume that you will now accept the faith of Judaism that people have moral freedom and can choose between right and wrong. This leaves us with our original question. How do we know that good is good? How do we know what ideals we should be guided by?

When Should We Be Intolerant of Differences?

We and our neighbors have all been brought up in certain ideals, which are shared by Judaism, Christianity and the democratic tradition which is inspired by them. Among these ideals are charity, honesty, justice and the love of peace. Perhaps these ideals seem self-evident to you and you have never thought of questioning them. But there have been groups with very different ideals, some of which appear completely evil to us. The Nazis regarded love of war as a virtue, and saw nothing wrong with hatred and brutality as long as they were directed to an "inferior race." And, if you read the newspapers, you know that the Communists don't regard individual freedom as a good thing.

We are convinced that we are right and that they are wrong. But they think the exact opposite. This is a very serious problem because it is concerned with the roots of our attitude to tolerance. As a general rule, we try to avoid intolerance. For example, the Hindu religion has many ceremonies that seem strange to us. We study them, try to understand them, and may even eventually learn that they are perfectly reasonable. But we do not for a moment tolerate ideas and practices like those of the Nazis. What then is the proper limit of tolerance? Where is tolerance right, and where is it wrong?

Perhaps we can get out of our difficulty if we distinguish between the two cases. One involves *moral principles* and the other their *application to particular situations*. Moral principles can never change, but their application can take hundreds of widely different forms.

The Importance of Moral Principles

The Nazis violated every moral principle any man has ever known. They not only violated Jewish principles but also Christian principles and the principles of our democratic way of life. No man can tolerate this.

Eastern civilizations, on the other hand, no matter how strange at first sight, do not always violate our moral principles. Their customs may seem exotic, and so may be their particular laws. But when we probe more deeply, with sympathy and understanding we often find the underlying moral principles to be similar to our own.

A specific example of how a moral principle can be applied in different ways is the question of capital punishment. The moral principle is law and order; but the application varies.

In some societies, there is no such thing as capital punishment. In other societies, its use is reserved as the penalty for murder. And in still other societies, capital punishment is inflicted for even minor crimes, such as petty theft. Which of these societies is right and which wrong?

The answer depends on the circumstances. In an ideal society, no punishment would be necessary at all. Today's most civilized nations have abolished capital punishment and there has been no increase in crime. In less advanced societies it is felt that capital punishment is needed to keep down the number of serious crimes. Finally, the third society may be so savage that the severest punishment for any crime is necessary to prevent the complete breakdown of law and order.

So all three societies have the right laws for their circumstances. The same principle—the maintenance of law and order—must be applied differently in different situations. Of course it is often hard to say how the principle should be applied in a given case.

The civilizations of ancient India, China, Israel and Greece were certainly very different from one another. But each of them independently discovered the Golden Rule. This indicates that at least some of the moral principles of these civilizations were the same. What differed was the application.

Since these unconnected civilizations arrived at the same moral standards, we must assume that man has a natural gift for moral insight very much like his gift for mathematical insight. You all know the Pythagorean Theorem—that in a right-angle triangle $A^2+B^2=C^2$. But perhaps you don't know that this theorem was separately discovered by the Babylonians and the Greeks. This demonstrates that man's mathematical reasoning is the same everywhere. And the Golden Rule shows the same thing about moral concepts.

Man Knows What Is Good

It is because of this universal gift that the Bible says man is created in the image of God. Of course, sometimes it takes a long time to develop moral insight, and some people have a hard time doing it, and there are even some who never succeed or who never really try. After all, when we say there is only one truth in mathematics, we don't deny that mathematics is difficult, and that we often make mistakes, and that some of us just don't or won't get it.

We can now solve the very difficult problem of the right and wrong kind of tolerance. You can and must be tolerant

"But you cannot and must not tolerate a wrong moral principle."

of someone trying to apply a moral principle in a new or different way. But you cannot and must not tolerate a wrong moral principle. When Hitler waged offensive war on peaceful nations and slaughtered millions of innocent people, he wasn't applying moral principles to an unusual situation; he was violating the principles in the worst way possible.

If you look into the Bible now, at certain passages with which you have been long familiar, such as the Ten Commandments or chapters in Amos and Isaiah, you will find that what you have learned here will give you a deeper understanding. You will no longer be shocked by the fact that much that is said in the Bible must be reinterpreted to be acceptable today; nor will you be surprised that so much can still be accepted quite literally. Much is no longer appropriate because the prophets had to adapt their teaching to the customs of ancient Israel. And much still is valid because it concerns moral principles rather than their applications. In these sections you will see that the depth of moral insight possessed by the prophets has rarely been equalled, and never excelled, in the entire history of mankind.

Chapter Eight: WHY DO WE PRAY?

One man prays for rain, the other for sun. Does God hear them both? Why then do we pray? How does prayer change us? When shall we pray, where shall we pray and with whom shall we pray? Who hears our prayer? Where is God when we pray?

"If we believe that God governs the universe according to the laws of nature, how can we believe that He will change these laws to suit our convenience?"

PRAYER aims at establishing communication between man and God. And prayer is of central importance in every phase of the Jewish religion. It is true that synagogue sermons are different from ordinary lectures, and Torah readings from ordinary study. For their aim is to change our attitudes and move us to action, instead of merely giving us information. But the awareness that we stand before God comes through prayer.

There are some questions about prayer that must be answered. One of these has to do with the purpose of prayer. If a sick person prays for health and then gets well, do you think his prayer is the cause of his recovery? If instead of getting well he dies, do you think that's because he didn't pray hard enough? If you think so, you might as well get rid of doctors and put all your trust in prayer.

Some people actually do this. Every now and then you read in the newspapers about a child who died because his parents refused medical aid and relied on prayer and faith alone. (Of course, the parents always insist that the child died because they didn't pray hard enough.)

Judaism does not condone such actions. Judaism believes in the fullest possible use of reason. If we trust our reason and experience, we know that prayer alone cannot cure cancer or tuberculosis, but that sometimes medical science can. To rely on prayer alone would be to pray for miracles.

To pray for miracles then, is irrational, because it is done with the idea of altering, through prayer, the course of nature. It is also irreligious. The religious man sees the world as an orderly creation of a good and wise God. Then how can he ask that God's order be changed? Such a prayer says that we know better than God.

Two Ways of Asking in Prayer

A world in which God granted everyone's wishes would have no order at all. During the summer in the country, farmers pray for rain for their crops and hotel owners pray for fair weather to attract more customers. Both are legitimate wishes. But to whom is God supposed to listen? If we believe that God governs the universe according to the laws of nature, how can we believe that He will change these laws to suit our convenience? On both scientific and religious grounds, this kind of prayer is unacceptable.

Does this rule out every kind of petitional prayer? But our prayer book is full of these—prayers for health and long life, mercy and forgiveness, justice and peace.

The truly pious Jew who says such petitional prayers has a completely different attitude from that of the farmer and the hotel owner. The pious man does not think of his prayer as a magical instrument with which to change the will of God. Hence when such a person's prayer is not granted, he does not accuse himself of not having prayed hard enough— nor does he lose faith in God. He has prayed for what he thought was best for him. When his prayer is not granted he does not despair, for he has faith and confidence that God's will will triumph in the end.

This is not an easy attitude to acquire. As the Book of Job shows, even the most pious person must often wrestle with doubts and overcome feelings of resentment. But until this attitude is acquired, we cannot fully experience the strength that religious faith brings to the believer. When the religious person seems to be praying for the fulfillment of his own wishes, he is actually praying for the fulfillment of God's purpose, not his own.

What Can Prayer Do for Us?

Perhaps you are wondering then, why we pray at all. Are not God's purposes accomplished whether we pray or not? The answer to this question brings us to the real meaning of prayer. We pray not to change God's purposes, but our own—so as to make them conform to God's. Having thus changed them, we become willing to act as God's co-workers. And this too is part of God's will. But it is not done for us. We can only do it ourselves, through prayer.

The religious person wants to change himself to conform to God. And through prayer he makes himself one with God. He is no longer self-centered but becomes God-centered.

The God-centered man no longer views the world merely in his own terms. He accepts life with complete trust in God's wisdom. He no longer feels separated from God, but united in love and understanding. This love of God is regarded in Judaism as one of the great accomplishments which life has to offer. It gives to the religious man an assurance of God's presence to sustain him even in times of pain and tragedy—perhaps above all in such times. Thus the real reason we pray is to be one with God.

There is a story about two children that helps us understand the difference between the wrong and the right kind of petitional prayer. The father of the first child is rich and very busy. He gives his child a lot of toys, but has no time to play with him. The father of the second is poor, and can't afford to buy toys. But he spends many hours each day with his child. The first child is rich—but poor. The second is poor—but rich.

When we pray to God for the things we want, we put ourselves in the position of the first child. Instead of seeking God's presence we are asking Him for gifts. But the gifts are truly meaningful only when there is love behind them. When we pray to God that His purposes may be realized, then we are in the position of the second child. When through prayer we feel the presence of God, we are able to bear serenely the hardships of life, and to find the strength to labor in His service.

There are considerable similarities between the God-man relationship in prayer, and certain human relationships, such as father to son or friend to friend. But there is also a great difference. For God is God, and not just a human friend or father. The person who truly prays experiences both a feeling of love and friendship toward God and also a deep sense of awe. The deeper his sense of awe the closer he is to the highest form of prayer—praise.

In the purest form of prayer we praise God spontaneously; we sing of God's glory. And, as you know, many Jewish prayers begin with the words "Praised be Thou...." In this way we are giving of ourselves to God.

The Purposes of Institutional Prayer

But how can we be spontaneous all the time? There are

times when we just can't pray, no matter how hard we try. It may seem that Judaism fails to recognize this fact for, as you know, Jews pray at fixed times. Thus we pray on the holidays, even if we don't feel in the right mood for it.

Actually, this is a very wise thing. The institution of prayer at fixed times is based on the insight that a person who disciplines himself to attempting prayer regularly has at least a chance that he may sometimes succeed. A holiday service, or any other service, has fulfilled its function if even one of the worshipers has spoken, in the right spirit, even a single prayer.

The Importance of Praying Together

But the Jew prays at fixed times for still another reason. He is called on to pray with others within a congregation. Of course it is impossible for every member of a congregation to feel like praying at the same time. So there have to be fixed times for the assembly to worship.

Perhaps you feel that, ideally, private prayer is best. At the same time, you have no doubt sometimes felt that being in the midst of a congregation is very often a real help. The presence of others engaged in prayer, the music and ritual, the Sabbath or Holy Day atmosphere—all these are vital aspects of prayer which are missing when you pray in solitude.

The congregation may also be an obstacle to prayer because congregations are sometimes noisy, and still more importantly because some prayers are completely between the individual and his God. This is why Judaism emphasizes public prayer but leaves room for private prayer as well.

103

But there is still another and far deeper reason why the Jew is called on to pray together with other Jews. Judaism asserts that most of our prayers ought to be spoken by a collective "we" rather than an individual "I." This is because God made a covenant with the whole Jewish people, not just with Abraham or Moses. No doubt you have noticed that in our prayer book the expression "our God" occurs very often, and "my God" only rarely. Also you know that while some of the prayers in the prayer book may be spoken by individuals, others may be spoken only when at least ten men are present.

This Jewish belief we will discuss further in Chapters X, XI and XII.

Where Is God When We Pray?

There is one more question about prayer which is really the biggest and most important of all. We have seen that in petitional prayer we communicate with God and thus gain strength and a sense of direction. We have also seen that in prayer of praise we joyously give thanks to God, and this too is a form of communication with Him. Finally we have seen that communication with God is aimed at by the whole congregation as well as by the individual. The remaining question is: How do we know that there ever really is a communication with God?

We may think we experience communication, but this might only be our own imagination. It is possible that we merely feel that God is present, without God actually being present. You will remember that we have already touched on this question on several occasions. But in connection with prayer it hits us with all its full force.

We cannot possibly prove that God is really present in prayer. The mere fact that we feel He is present doesn't prove He is present. On the other hand, we cannot disprove

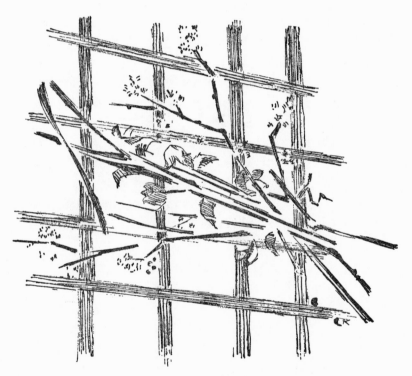

"We have also seen that in prayer of praise we joyously give thanks to God ..."

His presence. And thus the belief, while not based on reason, is not against reason either.

But why then accept this unprovable belief? Here the Jewish faith in a good God finds one of its biggest tests. A God who cannot be present to man isn't ultimately a good God, for He is impersonal and indifferent. He lacks love. The Jew who believes in the goodness of God believes that God loves him, that He is with us when we pray.

In committing himself to this belief, the religious Jew adds a whole dimension to his existence. You can't prove that human love is real either. Yet the person who believes love can be real enters into relationships with others, and thus finds the reality of love. The same is true of the religious Jew who prays. He enters into a relationship with God, and thus his belief in its reality is more and more confirmed. He can never prove that this relationship is real, but he doubts it less and less as his heart gets more and more attuned to prayer. And thus his life becomes more and more enriched, just as the lives of men become enriched by love.

Chapter Nine: ARE MEN IMMORTAL?

What happens to us when we die? When our bodies disintegrate, what happens to our minds or souls? Can we prove that there is such a thing as immortality? Have the Jews always believed that men are immortal? Why should we believe this?

"But if the spirit doesn't disappear, where does it go?"

MEN HAVE always wondered what happens to people when they die. We know that bodies disintegrate and change into other forms of matter. But what happens to the soul? The soul or spirit or mind of man is not material and therefore cannot turn into dust. From our experience, we know that nothing disappears completely. But if the spirit doesn't disappear, where does it go?

This question becomes very real and personal when someone very close to you dies. At one moment your grandfather or uncle or friend is still with you—and the next moment he is gone. It is very hard for us to accept this, and most of us cannot believe that nothing of the beloved person has survived. It seems almost necessary for us to feel that the person still exists, though where and in what form we cannot say.

Throughout history, the human imagination has created a great many stories about where people who die are and what has happened to them. Hell has always been described in terms of what was most painful and undesirable, and heaven in terms of the most extreme pleasure and happiness. Thus, to the Eskimoes, hell is a place of eternal cold. And to certain Eastern peoples, heaven is full of color and sensuous beauty.

The various beliefs about heaven and hell often reflect profound ideas, and it would be interesting to study and compare them. But in this chapter we are not interested in such a comparison—such as why some people think of hell as a cold place rather than as a hot place. All we care about is the truth or untruth of the belief in life after death.

The Immortality of the Body

Some people, Jews as well as Christians, believe that at the Day of Last Judgment every human body will be restored to life and reunited to its soul. Sometimes they base this belief on the 37th Chapter of Ezekiel. But if the matter of a human body has turned into other matter, how can it be restored to its original shape?

Jewish believers in bodily immortality were so deeply convinced that the body, being a gift of God, is good, that they were prepared to accept the difficult belief in the resurrection of the body. To make this belief acceptable, they said that resurrection could occur by divine miracle. Since God created the whole universe and all the life in it, surely it would be possible for Him miraculously to resurrect life.

The Immortality of the Soul

What we are going to talk about in this chapter, however, is not immortality of the body but immortality of the soul.

Does the mind or soul disintegrate at death the way the body does; that is, turn into matter? No, because then the mind would have to be matter in the first place, which it is not. Sometimes people think that the mind is the same thing as the brain, but this is a mistake. How many inches is your mind? How many pounds does it weigh? To ask such questions is to see immediately how silly they are. The mind can't be measured because it isn't material.

On the other hand, most of us cannot believe that the mind simply vanishes into nothingness. We find it very hard to believe that it vanishes without a trace, like the rabbit in the magician's hat.

Many Jewish thinkers have believed that the body as well as the soul is immortal. Other Jewish thinkers have held that the soul alone survives.

But no matter how strongly we hold either belief, we can never *prove* that even the soul continues to exist. For the afterlife is, as Hamlet says in Shakespeare's play, "the undiscovered country from whose bourne no traveller returns." And if that "country" exists, we cannot possibly imagine what it is like—until we get there. How can a disembodied soul think, feel, act, will? This is an unanswerable question. The wisest Jewish thinkers tell us to believe in an afterlife, but to refrain from speculating about what it is like.

But if we can't prove that afterlife exists, and if we can never know what it's like, why believe in it all? You may have heard that, in the earliest times, Judaism took just this position and refused to accept the belief in any form of afterlife.

Why Jews Believe in Afterlife

The early Jews believed that virtue was rewarded and vice punished in this life. They were convinced that each man succeeded or failed as he deserved. And so long as this was believed, there was no reason to accept the idea of an afterlife.

But it was soon discovered that virtue is not always rewarded in this life, and that vice often goes unpunished.

"The Jewish belief in immortality assures us that every life is complete, that death is not the final end."

Jeremiah and Job saw that sometimes in this life the wicked fare well and the innocent suffer terribly.

The moment they made this discovery, Jewish thinkers had to make a very important choice. They could either start believing in an afterlife or assume that God's world was unfair. What they did was to accept the belief in afterlife.

This was the choice they had to make. For as we have often stressed, the central belief of Judaism is an ultimate optimism, an unshakable conviction that in God's creation all things are ultimately good and right, even though it sometimes seems otherwise. It is in the case of death, above all, that this optimism is put to a test. When someone close to us dies, we almost always feel that his death was untimely. He didn't have the chance to do all he could have and should have done, and he wasn't given everything that we think he should have been given. In short, his life was not complete. The Jewish belief in immortality assures us that every life is complete, that death is not the final end.

Is the Belief in an Afterlife Wishful Thinking?

But isn't this belief, then, just a kind of wishful thinking? Isn't it only because we don't want life to remain incomplete that we believe in an afterlife? No.

Judaism doesn't picture afterlife as just pleasure and happiness. If everything that has remained incomplete is to be made complete, this doesn't mean only that we are given what we were denied in this life. It means also that we have to give an account of what we failed to do in life because of laziness or sin.

Judaism expresses this aspect with the idea of an ultimate divine judgment. Judaism never took hell seriously, for it could not believe that any man was such a terrible sinner as to deserve eternal damnation. At the same time, it always knew that no man was wholly free from sin. This is why it had to form the picture of a divine judgment which wipes the slate clean, as a necessary part of its picture of afterlife.

But another point is even more important. Certainly wanting something to be true doesn't make it true. On the other hand, a belief isn't false because we want it to be true. If that were so, every optimistic belief would be false.

Only shallow optimism is necessarily false—the kind which glosses over nasty, ugly, evil facts. The Jewish belief in afterlife does not do this. The Jew who accepts this belief faces up to everything that is evil and meaningless, and yet stubbornly believes that ultimately all things are well with God's world. When confronted by skeptics, he freely admits that he cannot prove this optimism. But he stakes his life on it.

But Judaism also tells us that afterlife is a mystery which we cannot possibly understand. This has always been the Jewish position, and it must be our position today. In the case of belief in an afterlife, more than in that of any other belief, reason is limited in its attempt to understand what faith accepts.

PART THREE

ISRAEL

Chapter Ten: WHY DO WE
REMAIN JEWS?

What is a Jew? Race? Religion? Nation? Nationality?
How has Judaism survived, even in modern times?
Why has the idea of a covenant with God been so im-
portant to us in the past? Can Jews today believe in
the covenant? Is anything wrong with the ideas of
Jews who do not believe in the covenant? Who made
the covenant, the Jews or God?

"We have survived for the sake of our mission, which comes
not from us, but from God."

BEFORE we can ask ourselves why we should go on being Jews we must determine what Jews are. What is a Jew?

One answer is that the Jews are a race. This answer may seem to be true, because you can often recognize that a man is a Jew by the way he looks. But there are many Jews who don't "look Jewish." And many people who do look Jewish are not Jews. The scientific study of race, which is called anthropology, teaches us that there is no such thing as a Jewish race.

In America, we often define Jews as the members of the Jewish religion. But many Jews do not believe in Judaism and have no connection with a synagogue or temple. Nevertheless these people call themselves Jews, and they are accepted as Jews by others, both Jews and non-Jews. Everyone who is born a Jew remains a Jew, unless he chooses to break away. And even then he often cannot.

A nation, too, consists of those who are born into it. But the people who belong to a nation share a common language, a common land and a common government. This is not true of the Jews except in Israel. Also, while there are at least two Jewish languages—Hebrew and Yiddish—many Jews do not speak or read either one.

By a nationality we mean a group of people united by history, traditions and (sometimes) a common language. This group can be spread over many nations and be composed of the citizens of many states. Are the Jews a nationality?

The Jews don't seem to be a nationality any more than they are a nation, a race or a religion. In the first place, the Jews have always accepted converts. A gentile who of his own free will embraces Judaism is considered a Jew in the full sense. After he accepts Judaism, the convert comes to share Jewish tradition and history.

Also, other nationalities tend to disappear when they move from their home soil, but this never happens to the Jews. A Pole who comes to the United States or Canada may preserve his traditions, and so may his son. But usually his grandson begins to forget about being Polish, and his great-grandson may have no reminder of Poland except his name, if he or his father hasn't changed it. He doesn't speak a word of Polish, and the culture of his great-grandfather means next to nothing to him.

Now the fourth or fifth generation American Jew may no longer speak Yiddish. And often he knows very little of Jewish culture. But in almost every case he is still a Jew—an American Jew. In many cases his gentile neighbors, whatever their national origin, consider themselves American—not Irish-American or Polish-American, but just American.

Jews have the Unique Ability to Survive

So we still haven't answered the question, "What is a Jew?" For none of the answers thus far given quite fits. There seems to be something unique about the Jew. What has made the Jewish people's past obviously different is their amazing ability to survive. The survival of the Jews is one of the mysteries of the ages. What was the reason for their survival?

The Covenant Was an Obligation to Survive

The history of the Jews, starting from the earliest Bible days, shows us that the chief reason for their survival was that they always believed themselves singled out by God for a special task and a special destiny. If the Israelites in Egypt had not held this belief, they never would have left Egypt. And if they had remained in Egypt, they would have become assimilated—that is, they would have become Egyptians and forgotten that they had ever been Israelites.

Since the time of Moses the Jews have had many other opportunities to assimilate to alien cultures. But the majority of Jews always refused to do this. In Babylon, in Alexandria, in Spain, in Europe and in America, the great majority of Jews have always remained faithful to the belief that they were obligated to God by an ancient covenant, the contract in which the Jews promised to obey the divine laws and God promised to watch over the destiny of the Jews.

Now we know something about the Jews of the past. They were not a religion or a race or a nation or a nationality. They were a people who considered themselves bound to God by a covenant. This is what a Jew was.

But some thinkers, even devout ones, find it hard today to accept the old idea of a covenant between God and man. Can we still believe in the old idea? And if not, is there any reason why we should go on being Jews?

It is certainly possible to say no to both these questions. There are some Jews who do say no and who believe it is no longer necessary or even desirable to remain Jews. Such Jews are called *assimilationists.*

"They were a people who considered themselves bound to God by a covenant."

Should the Jew Continue to Survive?

Can the assimilationist make a good case for his belief? Or does he just not like remaining Jewish and find reasons afterwards? Let us consider his case.

How does the assimilationist interpret the three thousand years of Jewish history, of which he is the product? He can say that Judaism is no longer needed because another religion (say, Christianity) is now doing the job once done by Judaism. This answer we shall consider in a later chapter.

Or the assimilationist can say that Judaism is no longer needed because its task is accomplished. No. For the task of Judaism is as needed today as it was in the time of Micah. Men still must learn to act justly, to love mercy, to walk humbly with their God.

Finally, the assimilationist can say that there never was a good reason for Jewish existence. He can say that the reasons accepted as good, such as that God once made a covenant with Israel, were nothing but primitive superstitions. Not only should the Jew of today assimilate, he should have done so at any time he had a chance. Had he done so, he would have spared himself and his descendants mountains of senseless grief.

The three thousand years of Jewish history are tragic enough, however they are viewed. But to the person who believes that Jewish existence is meaningful, it was worth all the tragedy. He knows that his ancestors dedicated themselves to a supremely valuable task, and that their magnificent accomplishment outweighed the suffering and sacrifice. For the assimilationist there can be no such compensation.

123

For him, Jewish history must be a meaningless tragedy. At the cost of incredible sacrifice, the Jews survived. Yet it was all for nothing! Jewish survival was a childish superstition, a silly mistake! Can anyone, even an assimilationist, really believe this?

The facts of history point in the opposite direction. National survival is not easy. The mighty empires of Egypt, Assyria, Babylonia, Greece and Rome all perished. The Jews were not a mighty empire—they were a tiny people dispersed among the nations—yet the Jew and his religious culture have survived until today.

This survival is so miraculous that many historians, including non-Jews, have felt that it cannot be explained except in terms of divine providence. Now the assimilationist comes along and tells us that this mighty faith, which succeeded where the greatest empires failed, is nothing but a primitive superstition, a childish error! It is much more likely that it is the assimilationist's theory that is childish and implausible.

Why should the Jew Continue to Survive?

There are other Jews who say we should go on being Jews, but merely because we have no choice. They say that assimilation never works, that antisemitism affects the Jew who has changed his name and religion just as much as the Jew who has remained a Jew. They are of course wrong. In most periods of history, the Jew who really wanted to assimilate could do it. And if he could not, his children or his grandchildren certainly could. The ten lost tribes were lost in just this way. And so we cannot remain Jews only because some people say Jews can never assimilate.

There are still other Jews who say that we ought to remain Jews because only in this way can we lead a happy and well-adjusted life. They say that everybody has to belong to a group if he is to feel happy and secure. They add that the Jew cannot really "belong" to non-Jewish groups. He can join them, but he does not feel emotionally at home. It is only in Jewish groups that he feels truly at ease. If he steeps himself in Jewish culture, literature and music, he sinks his roots deeply and well. But if he tries to break away from his Jewishness, that is a sure sign of emotional maladjustment. And this maladjustment cannot be cured by moving into another group. He can only straighten himself out by strengthening, rather that weakening, his ties with Jewishness.

This view has great merits. It also has some weaknesses. The merit is that it stresses the positive content of Jewish life. It reminds us that Jewish history has not been simply a history of tragedies and persecutions. This group has been largely responsible for the revival of interest in the rich culture of the East European ghetto, with its laughter and humanity as well as its tears. In the study of this culture and other Jewish cultures of the past, the Jew of today finds much to copy, and much in which he still feels at home.

Still, the view that we ought to remain Jews in order to be happy and well-adjusted has one main weakness. Suppose a Jew is in a situation where he cannot be happy and well-adjusted within the Jewish group. Should he then stop being a Jew? And suppose he can become happy and well-adjusted within another group. Is it right for him to assimilate?

In America today, these are vital questions. There are many non-Jewish groups in this country in which Jews are welcomed and in which they can feel at home. And in small towns in some areas—such as the South—there are often only one or two Jewish families and therefore, of course, no Jewish group. If the chief aim in life is happiness and adjustment, there is no good reason why Jews in such situations should not assimilate as quickly and effectively as possible. And this is why this argument is not reason enough for us to remain Jews.

The True Purpose in Jewish Survival

But there is a far deeper reason for the inadequacy of this view. While Jewish existence has its enjoyable aspects, it is clearly not all joy. The Jew who lives in America may not always remember this, but the Jew who lived at other times and in other countries could never forget it. In times of persecution it was certainly not fun to be Jewish, and if Jews had been in search of nothing but comfort, they would long ago have abandoned their faith. They remained Jewish because they remembered the covenant, their sacred obligation. And unless we too can believe that to remain Jews is a sacred obligation, our reasons for being Jewish will be weak indeed. Without this strengthening faith we would be fairweather Jews, ready to abandon our Jewishness at the first hint of storms ahead.

Jews who feel that they have an obligation to remain Jews believe that the Jewish people has a mission. It was among

Jews that the belief in one God first arose. It was among Jews, too, that certain moral beliefs first arose. These are the beliefs that govern modern society at its best—the belief in justice for all, in loving one's neighbor, and in universal peace as the ultimate aim toward which we all ought to strive. Those who believe in a Jewish mission maintain that, while everyone is obligated to follow these principles, the Jew has a special obligation. The Jew's special obligation, his mission, is to keep on believing and practicing God's word. Sometimes people forget. This is why the Jew is obligated to remain a Jew.

The Jew cannot forget; he must not. His tradition is too long and too deep to allow him to do so. He cannot forget the words of Moses. He cannot forget the words of the prophets, nor of the rabbis who followed them. The Jew cannot plead ignorance.

We have now answered our question. The Jewish mission is the only completely positive reason we can offer for remaining Jews. But it is still not easy to accept the idea that God chose us, the Jews, a small humble group, to live by His word throughout all generations.

Who Made the Covenant?

Some people today think that God never chose the Jews; that, instead, the Jews chose God. They say that the Jewish mission of ethical monotheism was a discovery of our ancestors just as geometry was a discovery of the ancient Greeks. This is at first an attractive idea, because we don't have to accept the belief that God interfered with the course of history in order to choose Israel for a special mission.

Also, they find it is presumptuous for Jews to believe that God Himself should give them His special attention, and single them out for a special task.

Perhaps one could say that our ancestors were pious and dedicated enough to choose God. But can we say the same thing of Jews throughout history—and of ourselves today? If we regard Judaism as wholly man-made, we would have to account for the miraculous survival of our people in terms of their dedication and piety alone. But can we really say in all honesty and humility that we are all that superior in these qualities to other peoples that have not survived? It seems that it is the belief that the Jews chose God which is really presumptuous. While the Jewish tradition claims a special mission for all the Jewish people, it makes no extravagant claims for their gifts and accomplishments. On the contrary, the Torah repeatedly characterizes the Jews as a stiff-necked people.

The Bible condemns the moral laxness of the Jews and points out the imperfections of Jewish leaders and prophets. Almost every prophet mentioned in the Bible shrinks from assuming his God-given destiny because of his sense of his moral shortcomings. And even Moses, the greatest of the prophets, was not allowed to enter the Holy Land because he himself was not free from sin. But if Moses, the prophets and the people were all that imperfect, how can they have achieved so much? You can find the answer in the Bible itself. Moses and the prophets always knew that their message came to them, not as the result of their superior insight, but as a revelation from God—and this has been the traditional Jewish view at all times.

It may be much easier to leave God out of the picture, and to believe that Judaism is wholly man-made. But if this is true, how can we believe that we have a unique mission, without asserting intolerably arrogant claims?

God Made the Covenant

In the end, we too are driven to the traditional belief that God is the author of our mission. We then truly believe that it is God whose ancient covenant we keep. Then we can humbly confess our human weaknesses and still maintain our faith in our sacred mission. We have survived for the sake of our mission, which comes not from us, but from God.

Chapter Eleven: WHY ARE THERE
DIVISIONS IN JUDAISM?

*All religious Jews believe in Torah. But what do we
mean by "believe"? What does the Orthodox Jew
believe? What does the non-Orthodox Jew believe?
Who wrote the Bible—God or man? What do we mean
when we say that the Bible was divinely inspired? A
way of life can be a way of worshiping God. Orthodoxy has its way. Conservatism has its way. Reform
has its way.*

*"They believe that the Jews never would have survived through
all these centuries if they did not have a way of living . ."*

J UDAISM on the North American continent is divided into three groups: Orthodox, Conservative and Reform. In this chapter we are going to describe the differences between them and try to find out why each group believes and behaves as it does.

Everyone knows that Orthodox Jews wear hats in the synagogue and conduct their services in Hebrew. They eat only kosher food, and will neither ride nor light fires on the Sabbath. Reform Jews, on the other hand, do not wear hats in the temple, and they conduct their services mostly in English. Few of them observe the kosher food laws, and none of them refrain from riding or lighting fires on the Sabbath. The behavior of Conservative Jews resembles that of the Orthodox while they are in the synagogue, but in daily life they act more like Reform Jews.

Part of the Reform argument for abolishing the old laws is that they are out of date. For instance, thousands of years ago, when the laws were made, you had to work to light a fire, and you had to make a horse work if you wanted to ride. But today there is no labor involved for man or animal in turning on an electric switch or in driving a car. Also, they say the laws against eating pork were sensible when the Bible was written, because at that time pork often caused trichinosis. But with today's hygienic farming, plus governmental inspection, pork can be as safe and healthful as any other meat.

Orthodoxy's Simple Truth

If this is so, then why do people stay Orthodox? What does an intelligent and enlightened Orthodox Jew say to the Reform arguments?

The Orthodox Jew would say that the Torah was given to us by God. God knew that conditions would change. Nevertheless, He gave the Torah for all time. And the Orthodox Jew says that because the Torah comes from God, we must always obey it, even when we don't understand its purpose.

But this basic Orthodox belief cannot be proved. It is said many times in the Torah that the Torah is God-given. But this is a proof only to someone who believes that every word in the Torah is literally true.

The Orthodox Jew cannot prove his central belief, but no one can disprove it either. For example, non-Orthodox scholars have tried to disprove the divine origin of the Book of Isaiah by saying that Isaiah did not write all of the book. They point out that some chapters in Isaiah tell about the destruction of the Temple, although Isaiah lived a hundred years before that event. Orthodox Jews say that this only means that Isaiah was inspired by God and had knowledge of the future.

So we see that there are divisions of belief in Judaism because no one can prove or disprove that every word in the Bible is from God.

Is Orthodoxy Impossible?

Another reason for the differences is that some Jews say that today it is impossible to live according to the old laws. They say that it is impossible to be an Orthodox Jew. For example, if Israeli farmers did not milk their cows on the Sabbath, they would ruin their farms and destroy the economy of the whole country. Or, to take an even more dramatic example, no one today would dream of observing the Biblical injunction, *An eye for an eye, a tooth for a tooth.*

But these are not true examples of Orthodox practice. Orthodox Judaism has never been that rigid. Indeed, Orthodox rabbis have often interpreted the Torah with astonishing freedom and adaptability. They are able to do this because Orthodoxy believes in the "oral Torah" as well as in the "written Torah." According to tradition, when God gave Moses the Torah, He gave him additional instruction by word of mouth. From Moses, this oral teaching passed from generation to generation, until it, too, was written down in the Talmud.

Orthodoxy offers ways to adapt the "impossibilities" of Orthodox Judaism to the necessities of life. For instance, it interprets "an eye for an eye" in a way completely acceptable to our moral consciousness. It says that if someone damages another's eye, he must pay a sum of money equal to the value of the eye. (This is probably the way in which the Biblical statement itself must be understood.) Orthodox Jews have also found an interpretation of the laws that permits the milking of cows on the Sabbath. Therefore, while it is definitely difficult to live by the Orthodox law, it is not impossible. Conservative and Reform Jews may disagree with Orthodoxy; but they cannot dismiss it as unintelligent or unworkable.

Earlier we showed that while some Jews took the Torah as the word of God, others did not. The moment we believe

"Therefore, while it is definitely difficult to live by the orthodox law, it is not impossible."

that the Torah could have been a human product, it becomes our right, perhaps even our duty, to reinterpret it.

The central purpose of the Torah is to teach us how to lead the good life. And for the Orthodox Jew, the only way to do this is to obey the 613 God-given commandments. But for the non-Orthodox, the path is not so simple. He must first ask if these laws still serve the central purpose. And if they don't, then he must change these laws or stop observing them.

Moral Laws and Ceremonial Laws

The non-Orthodox Jew has found that a whole group of laws are not concerned with the good life, with morality. There is nothing moral (or immoral) about not eating pork, or wearing a hat in synagogue, or conducting services in Hebrew. We call this kind of law "ritual" or "ceremonial."

At one time, a radical wing of Reform Judaism dropped this whole class of laws. These extremist Reform Jews believed that ritual is a holdover from the past and has no useful function today. They felt that if they got rid of these external ceremonies they would be left with the pure essence of Judaism—ethical monotheism.

There are still Reform Jews today who take this radical view, but far fewer than fifty years ago. In recent years, even in Reform, there has been a growing emphasis on tradition. Reform services tend more and more to be conducted partly in Hebrew. And many Reform Jews are returning to ancient practices, such as lighting candles on Friday night.

One reason for this turning back to ritual is the feeling that it is a powerful help toward living the good life. The good life itself consists in living by the moral laws, but ceremonies can lead us in the right direction. We cannot behave morally without self-discipline, and traditional laws concerning fasting or praying in Hebrew at fixed periods help achieve self-discipline. It is all very well for a person to say he will pray whenever the spirit moves him; but we know from experience that unless he sets fixed times, the spirit may never move him.

Of course, this is not the whole story. There are more complicated cases in which the observance of a law may hurt the good life instead of helping it. If a man studies Hebrew with love and patience, his religious life will be greatly enriched if he prays in Hebrew. But if someone does not understand the language, his Hebrew prayer may be completely empty of meaning. Or one man may attain a deep sense of the sanctity of Yom Kippur by fasting. But the man who spends all that day thinking only of food should not have fasted in the first place.

Shall we keep Hebrew in the services, or drop it? Shall we fast on Yom Kippur, or eat? It is difficult, if not impossible, to arrive at "correct" answers, and Conservative and Reform Jews (even among themselves) frequently disagree on these questions.

And so we see that even when we try to change the laws to guide us in the good life today, there is no one way of changing them.

Ceremonies Keep the Jews Together

But keeping the ceremonial laws has still another purpose. It not only serves moral ends, but it also keeps the Jews together as a people. We know that it is necessary for the Jews to remain a separate entity if they are to fulfill the mission of Israel. The radical Reform Jews believe that the Jews can maintain their identity simply by remaining faithful to their beliefs. But all other Jews believe that ritual is necessary, too. They believe that the Jews never would have survived through all these centuries if they had not had a way of living—of eating and dressing and speaking and praying —which was different from all others, and distinctively Jewish.

The Torah Is Divinely Inspired

We have seen that the differences of belief about whether the Torah was written by God or man have led to differences in observance. The Orthodox belief is simple to understand. The Torah was written by God and there is no question about it. All its laws must be followed. The non-Orthodox belief is not so simple and must be examined more closely.

The non-Orthodox Jew believes that the Torah was written partly by men. But he believes that the men who helped write the Torah were inspired by God. This idea may seem strange at first, but you are familiar with it even outside of religion as the idea of "inspiration." Often an artist or composer will produce his best work suddenly, without a moment's thought. He calls this "inspiration," and sometimes believes that it comes from God. The Bible is a work of such magnificent greatness that it is natural for the non-Orthodox Jew to believe it was written under divine inspiration.

The Importance of Believing in Divine Inspiration

It is tremendously important for us to believe that the Torah is divinely inspired. If we believe that the Torah is completely the work of human beings, then it is just another book, no matter how precious its teachings. But if it is the direct inspiration of God, this shows that God is not a distant, impersonal force, but that He dwells in our midst. You may have experienced this profound aspect of Judaism personally—when there was a moment, during a service or a Friday night meal or in camp around the fire, which seemed hallowed and sacred—one of those quiet moments when you forget everything else and are aware only of the presence of God.

When we believe that the Torah is inspired by God, and we follow its commandments, each and every daily act becomes a way of worshiping Him. Even when we eat our bread, it becomes a ceremony. It is not only eating; it is also worshiping God.

When we accept the fact that the commandments in the Torah are divinely inspired, they become not only a means to moral perfection and survival, but also an end in themselves. They are in themselves a way of worshiping God.

Judaism has always held that we should praise and communicate with God by deeds as well as words, in the marketplace as well as in the synagogue. Judaism must be a total way of life.

Non-Orthodox Jews who believe in the divine inspiration of the Torah feel they are being true to tradition. Some non-Orthodox Jews feel that divine inspiration did not cease when the Torah was finished, that it has been with the people of Israel throughout their history. Whenever they make an attempt to adapt the teachings of the Torah to the conditions of our own time, they pray and hope for divine guidance. This has a parallel in traditional Judaism which believed that the Talmudic teachers had divine guidance when they interpreted the Torah.

Differences Among Non-Orthodox Jews

So far, we have considered Reform and Conservative Judaism together, as distinguished from Orthodoxy. The reason for this treatment is that there is a sharp difference between Orthodoxy and non-Orthodoxy; but between Conservatism and Reform there is only a variation in emphasis.

Reform Judaism has always stressed that the one God of Judaism is the God of all mankind. The moral laws of Judaism are valid for all nations, and Israel's mission is in behalf of the whole human race. This philosophy is called *universalism*. The universalist elements have of course always been an essential part of Judaism. But during the centuries of ghetto life, when the Jews were cut off from other people, the universalist ideas were sometimes understressed, or even forgotten. When the Jew emerged from the medieval ghetto in the nineteenth century, the universalist ideas came to life again in Reform Judaism.

Conservative Judaism stresses the element of historical continuity. Conservatism stresses that traditions have helped hold the Jews together. It believes that strict following of old customs is not good, but it believes in a living tradition which changes according to the needs of the time. Therefore Conservative Judaism has concentrated on keeping alive much of the Jewish religious tradition, including its customs, ceremonies and folklore.

But it must not be thought that this difference between Reform and Conservative Judaism is more than a difference in emphasis. On the one hand, even the most radical wing in Reform Judaism has never wholly denied that Judaism must have a living tradition if it is to continue to exist. On the other hand, Conservative Judaism has always affirmed that the Jewish religion has a universal message for all men. Indeed, some students of the present Jewish scene have predicted that a time will come when Reform and Conservative Judaism will merge. Whether or not this prediction is correct, only time can tell. At present, each division fulfills a function essential to the preservation of Judaism. Each Jew must decide for himself his branch of Judaism. But whichever he chooses, he should be glad that the others exist.

Chapter Twelve: ON WHAT DO JEWS
AND CHRISTIANS DISAGREE?

Is Judaism the only true religion? Why do we believe that there can be other valid religions? What do Christians think about this? Who was Jesus? Why is he called a mediator for God? Do Jews believe in a mediator? Which is the best belief? Is it all a matter of faith?

" . . . Admit that the other fulfills a unique role . . ."

THROUGHOUT HISTORY the Jews have always been a minority. Even in ancient Palestine they were surrounded by a non-Jewish majority. This fact in itself means nothing. Spiritual truth cannot be established by counting noses. The Jews of ancient Palestine were convinced of the superiority of their religion over that of the pagans, which called for the worship of idols and which permitted human sacrifice.

But modern Christianity and modern Islam create a very special problem for Jews today. They share the monotheistic beliefs and most of the moral ideals of Judaism. So the truly religious and enlightened Jew today finds it necessary to respect Christianity and Islam, unlike the ancient Jew who could not respect paganism.

In this chapter we will discuss Christians and Jews, since it is among Christians that we live.

Most Christians claim that theirs is the only true religion. This is very disturbing for the followers of other religions because, if the Christian claim is true, other religions must all be false. In particular, it is disturbing for Jews. For Christianity regards itself as the fulfillment and completion of Judaism.

The Jew rejects the Christian claim regarding Judaism by remaining a Jew. He finds in Judaism the supreme expression of ethics and morality, of love of God and of concern for his fellow man. At the same time, Judaism shares much with Christianity, and the Jew cannot but have regard for this religion. So the problem is to discover the exact Christian beliefs with which the Jew disagrees, as well as the basis for the Jewish attitude.

Let us begin solving this problem by clearing up some common errors about the differences between the two religions. These errors are often due to ignorance or to bitter experiences. Jews have often been persecuted in Christian countries. This fact has made many Jews adopt a very negative attitude toward Christianity as a whole. The truth is, of course, that Christianity is deeply opposed to persecution in every form, and that anyone who persecutes cannot call himself a true Christian. Christians are often unfair toward Judaism because of ignorance and error. Since Judaism has fewer followers, it is not well known, and consequently even learned Christians are often ignorant of its profound teachings.

The Emphasis on Love

Perhaps the most frequent misunderstanding is that Judaism is only a religion of justice, while Christianity is a religion of love. This mistaken view is often supported by quoting a saying of Jesus to his followers. Jesus said to love your neighbors and to love God. But Jesus is actually quoting the Hebrew Bible (*Leviticus 19:18* and *Deuteronomy 6:5*). Judaism does emphasize love. The Deuteronomy passage is part of the Sh'ma, the principal declaration of belief of every Jew.

Christianity differs from Judaism by pushing the idea of love to a radical extreme. In the famous Sermon on the Mount, Jesus asks his followers to love their enemies. If your enemy hits your right cheek, says Jesus, then turn your left cheek to him. But even for this argument we can quote

Isaiah who said, "Say, 'Ye are our brethren,' to those who hate you." And similar ideas were expressed among the rabbis of Jesus' time, such as Hillel. But very few Christians know anything about Hillel.

Certainly a literal interpretation of the Sermon on the Mount could never be accepted by Judaism. According to Judaism, it is our duty to oppose evil. If a man like Hitler is not stopped as soon as possible, he will harm others as well as us. Our Bible specifically forbids us to stand by while the blood of our neighbors is being shed.

But very few Christians interpret the Sermon on the Mount literally. They, too, believe that armed resistance to evil is sometimes necessary. Most Christians interpret the famous sermon as a lesson to love the enemy. But they will fight against him when he is actively evil. When interpreted in this way, there is no conflict with Judaism.

The Christian Belief in Jesus

The real and inescapable difference between the two religions is the Christian claim that Jesus was the Messiah, and even the son of God.

Since the days of the prophets, the Jews had been waiting for a man, endowed by God with extraordinary powers, who would unite all men in love and brotherhood. This longed-for figure was called the Messiah. The hope for the Messiah has been a part of Judaism since then. Jews have believed that through his coming, good eventually will triumph over evil. But while in some ages the Jews have envisioned the Messianic age as a period in the far future,

147

at other times the entire Jewish people believed that the Messiah's coming was near. And in such times it often happened that an individual became sincerely convinced that he was the Messiah. If such an individual was a powerful and impressive personality, he often convinced others of the truth of his claim.

The time of Jesus was one of these times. Many of the people were swept with a spiritual excitement, certain that they were living in the "last days" which would witness the coming of the Messiah. No doubt Jesus himself was convinced that he was the long-awaited deliverer.

His message, too, was impressive. It addressed itself, above all, to those to whom the Messianic message would be most meaningful—the poor, the sick, the downtrodden. It promised them a better life in the world to come. And it was delivered with the kind of strength which flows only from an unfaltering faith. It is little wonder that many Jews, suffering as they did under the yoke of Roman oppression, should have seen in Jesus the long-expected Messiah—or that the Romans, seeing in him a potential danger to their oppressive empire, should have put him to death.

After the crucifixion of Jesus, nothing in the outside world changed. The Roman Empire remained with all its oppressiveness and cruelty and misery. Men did not beat their swords into plowshares and their spears into pruning hooks. The poor were still poor, and hatred had not turned into love. The Messiah had not yet come.

This was the view adopted by the vast majority of Jews, even of those who had regarded Jesus as the Messiah while he was still alive. But a small minority stuck to their belief that Jesus had indeed been the Messiah. They claimed that the world was the same outwardly, but that inwardly and spiritually it was redeemed. The good world promised by the prophets, according to this minority, was meant to be understood symbolically—and the symbolic promises had been fulfilled by the death of Jesus on the cross. These people were the first Christians.

Those who remained Jews were certain of their belief that as long as evil is practiced between man and man, or even between man and beast, the world is unredeemed. And this is the Jew's belief today.

The story is told of a Chassidic rabbi who had moved to Jerusalem in order to be present in case the Messiah should come. One day a practical joker went to the top of the Mount of Olives and blew a shofar—the expected sign of the arrival of the Messiah. In great excitement the rabbi rushed to the window to gaze upon the redeemed world. But the first thing he saw was a coachman beating his horse. This was enough to make him conclude sadly that the world was still unredeemed.

The Christian Explanation of Jesus as Messiah

The Jews who became Christians now had to explain why war, oppression and hate still held sway in the redeemed world. This was the beginning of Christian thinking and its divergence from Judaism. Christians came to believe that after Adam's sin, the original sin inherited by all mankind, there had been a tragic gulf between man and God. The sacrifice of Jesus on the cross then reconciled man with God. They argued that Jesus, who had achieved this reconciliation, could not have been a mere man. Jesus was now seen by the Christians as more than the human Messiah of Jewish tradition; they believed that he was God Himself, who in His love for man had assumed flesh and suffered the highest sacrifice for man's sake.

Christians still believe that God once made a covenant with Israel, which was to remain binding until all mankind was redeemed. But they believe that redemption has come. They hold that the covenant is no longer in force and that Israel's mission on earth is completed. Therefore, it is easy to see why Christians believe that there is no further reason for the continued existence of the Jews as a separate people and a separate religion.

But it is just as easy to see why the Jew should steadfastly insist on his continued separateness. He still sees the evil in the world. He still believes that the world has to learn the ways of God and that the Jewish mission still exists. This is an essential difference between Judaism and Christianity. For Christianity asserts that the world is already redeemed, and that hence the Jew's role has come to an end.

But even this difference is not as great as it seems. It is true that there are some Christians who seem to accept the evils of the world, such as poverty, oppression and war, because they believe that this world is important only as a place in which a man may, through Jesus, save his soul. But there are other Christians who have a different attitude.

These Christians believe that the coming of Jesus only began the work of redemption, and that its total fulfillment

—the "second coming"—will include the final realization of peace and justice in this world. They are also much more prepared to say that the Jewish mission is not yet wholly complete, and will not be so until redemption itself is complete. Christians of this kind always have been in the forefront of those fighting for justice and peace, and their view is much closer to the Jewish belief.

Christians Believe in a Mediator for God

Indeed, so close is their belief to that of Judaism that one is inclined to ask what crucial differences remain. To this question even the second kind of Christian will reply that the Jew may sincerely seek God but he cannot find Him. To find God man needs the mediator in the person of Jesus. This is of course the reason why Christians end their prayers with the expression, "through Jesus Christ, our Lord."

It is this answer which the Jew must reject with all the emphasis at his command. According to Judaism, there is no need for a mediator between God and man. Every man can always find Him, if he only seeks Him with all his heart.

It is true, as Christianity asserts, that man separates himself from God through sin, and the story of Adam illustrates this separation. But the Jewish view is that separation is never final, and man can always return to union with God. The Hebrew word for this return is *T'shuvah*, and Yom Kippur is dedicated to *"T'shuvah."* The holiest of Jewish Holy Days is devoted to the spiritual effort of returning to God. This illustrates how seriously the Jew takes man's sinful separation from God. But it also illustrates his belief that such a return is possible without the aid of a mediator.

"*According to Judaism...every man can always find Him, if he only seeks Him with all his heart.*"

But the Christian might still say that without a mediator no one can return so completely to God as to be wholly free of evil thoughts, evil passions, restlessness and inner war. The Jew replies that the Christian cannot achieve such a union with God, with or without the help of a mediator. Not until the Messianic days will the work of redemption be complete.

A Matter of Faith

Now we have reached a point of radical disagreement. It is a point which cannot be argued, because both sides are grounded in commitments deeper than logic. For two thousand years there have been men of immense intellectual ability who have argued whether or not men need a mediator to reach God.

We must remember two things in order to understand the Jewish position toward Christianity. First, Judaism is not a missionary religion. Jews have rarely tried to convert non-Jews to Judaism, though if a non-Jew sincerely wants to become Jewish he is accepted. While Judaism considers itself a true religion, it does not consider itself the only true religion. According to tradition, God gave 613 laws to Israel and, through Noah, He gave seven laws to all mankind. Jews believe that a gentile who observes these seven laws—the basic laws of morality—is just as beloved of God as a Jew who observes all 613.

Secondly, we as Jews can assign a very special place to Christianity, as a religion which directs its followers into righteous paths. In the end what Jew and Christian share is far more than what they disagree on. They share, not only the basic laws of morality and the belief in the One God, but also the belief that God is concerned with man, and that man ought to be concerned with God. They share the belief that the world stands in need of being redeemed, and that it ultimately will be redeemed. They share, perhaps above all, the belief that redemption, if and when it is finally achieved, must be the union of men, through love, with God as well as with each other.

Thus, ultimately, Jew and Christian may each disagree with the way the other understands his own position in history. But there is no reason why each should not admit that the other is a part of the fulfillment of God's purpose for the world and man.

CONCLUSION

W E HAVE now reached the end of our investigation. We have talked about God, about man, about Judaism which is our faith. And still we may wonder: "What now? As Jews, what is our part in the world of today?"

There is a statement in the Haggadah that we read every year at Passover. This statement sums up the whole of Jewish existence. It is a clue to the Jewish past, and a guide for the Jewish future. It says:

> *Each man in Israel, in every generation, shall consider himself as though he, too, had been brought forth from Egypt.*

What does the statement mean?

It means that Jews everywhere have always remembered their past and have sought to keep the past alive in the present. The Jewish people had a unique beginning. The Jewish people was born when it heeded something it could not touch and could not see—a Voice which bade it listen and follow. That Voice was audible only to the ear of faith, and those who heard it came up from slavery and became the Jewish people. The people and the faith were born together. They were inseparable, and have remained so.

What was it the people heard, and then heard again and again throughout the generations? It was a divine commandment. The commandment said that this world—disunited, rent by conflict, full of evil—was not what God meant it to be. It said that the world would some day be one, even as God is One, and that the Jewish people would play a special role in leading the world to its divine destiny. The Jewish people understood this, and tried to live by the commandment.

But where did the people gather strength to carry out the commandment? From a divine promise which assured the Jews that God would be with them always. God would never forsake them, even when they were weak, but would always be present with His succor and love.

Countless times the Jews were close to despair and nearly forsook the ancient covenant. But countless times they remembered the divine promise, and regathered strength to follow the divine commandment. Thus each Jew, even to-day, is reminded by the Haggadah that he, too, was brought forth from Egypt, as were his ancestors.

Is the ancient faith a mere irrationality, a dream? And, if so, is the Jewish people, who has been nourished on this faith, only an irrationality, only a dream? Certainly the skeptics have always felt this way and have many times declared the Jewish people to be dead and buried. But the Jewish people still exists, despite the skeptics, after thousands of years.

In this book we have tried to discover what good reasons we could for the central beliefs in Judaism. We have found that the Jewish faith is never contrary to reason. In fact, reason can often give it strong support. Reason tells us that there can be only one God, and not many gods. Good sense tells us that justice and love are better than evil.

But we have also found that there is more to our religion than "good sense." There is also passion and believing trust; there is faith. We believe not merely with our heads, but with our hearts which are open to the presence of God.

Modern civilization is not a civilization of faith. What then of the Jew today? We who live in modern times are tempted to forget about Egypt—more tempted than any of our ancestors. But the ancient memory still lingers; we cannot deny the past. Perhaps there is that greater Power who remembers the commandment and the promise and who will not let us forget.

If we listen, we Jews of today can still hear the echo of the Voice that called to the children of Israel. We can still choose to heed it. If and when we do, the ancient faith will be reborn in us and we shall resume the age-old journey. For we can still travel, even in the 20th century, the ancient road that has no end—until all that God has planned for the world will be fulfilled.